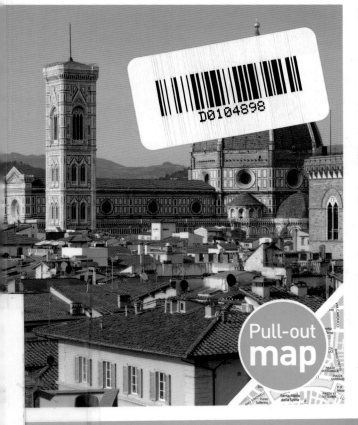

DK EYEWITNESS TRAVEL

TOP 10 2019

FLORENCE & TUSCANY

PALACES AND GARDENS ■ MUSEUMS AND GALLERIES
CAFES AND BARS ■ HILL TOWNS AND VINEYARDS
ITINERARIES AND WALKS ■ RESTAURANTS ■ HOTELS

Pull-out map

D0104898

YOUR GUIDE TO THE **10 BEST** OF EVERYTHING

How to Use the Maps

This Top 10 Travel Guide to Florence & Tuscany divides the region into eight areas, as shown below: Florence, Around Florence, Siena, Eastern Tuscany, Northwestern Tuscany, Western Hill Towns, Southern Tuscany, and the Southern Coast and Maremma.

- Each map inside the book has numbered dots marking the highlights
- Each itinerary has its own easy-to-follow map
- The pull-out map shows Florence and Tuscany at a larger scale

Area by Area Maps

To locate a sight, store, or restaurant on the area maps, use the color-coded dots.

④ Monte Argent
MAP E6 ■ Tourist

To locate a sight on the inside cover maps and pull-out map, use the grid references.

The pull-out map in the back cover pocket gives you the maps on the inside covers at a larger scale, plus indexes to Florence and Tuscany, and maps of Siena and Pisa.

Maps on the Inside Covers

Inside back cover shows an enlarged area of central Florence.

Map of Italy

Enlarged map on back cover

Inside front cover shows the whole of Tuscany.

Color-Coded Areas

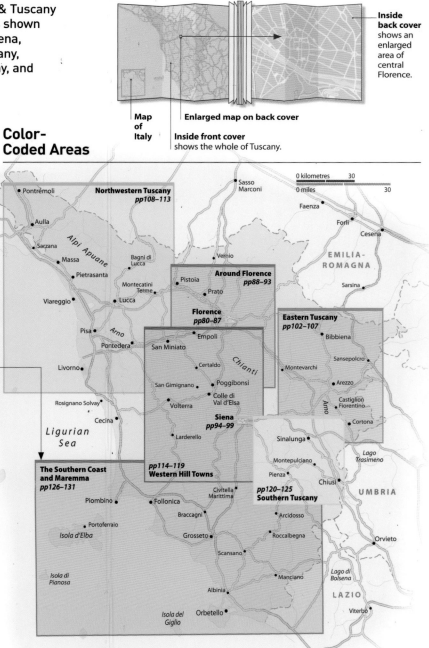

DK EYEWITNESS TRAVEL

TOP 10

FLORENCE & TUSCANY

REID BRAMBLETT

Penguin
Random
House

Top 10 Florence and Tuscany Highlights

The Top 10 of Everything

CONTENTS

Florence and Tuscany Area by Area

Streetsmart

Within each Top 10 list in this book, no hierarchy of quality or popularity is implied. All 10 are, in the editor's opinion, of roughly equal merit.

Front cover and spine *The Duomo Santa Maria del Fiore and Giotto's Bell Tower, Florence*
Back cover *Podere Belvedere near San Quirico d'Orcia, Siena*
Title page *Copy of Michelangelo's David in Piazza della Signoria*

Welcome to
Florence
and Tuscany

Florence's Piazza della Signoria as the morning sun hits the Palazzo Vecchio. A distant ridge dotted with cypress trees. A sizzling Chianina steak fresh from the flame grill. It is for these moments, and many more, that travellers have been visiting Tuscany for centuries. With Eyewitness Top 10 Florence & Tuscany, it's yours to explore.

At its heart sits **Florence**, city of the Renaissance and buzzing home to modern style icons like Gucci and Ferragamo. Here you'll discover many of the world's great paintings and sculptures, including those in the masterpiece-packed **Uffizi**, **Accademia** and **Pitti Palace**. In the shadow of Brunelleschi's iconic **Duomo dome** are cobblestoned streets upon which Dante and Michelangelo walked.

Beyond the Florence city limits are hill towns like **San Gimignano**, with stone towers and twisting alleys barely changed since the 1300s. **Siena** is a treasure-trove of paintings left by the trailblazers of Western art, while **Pisa** has the world's most photographed bit of botched architecture in one of Italy's most photogenic piazzas. The sublime landscapes of the **Chianti** and **Val d'Orcia** regions change dramatically with the passing of the seasons.

Whether you're coming for a weekend or a week, our Top 10 guide is designed to bring together the best of everything Tuscany can offer, from the hip, contemporary restaurants of **San Frediano** in Florence to the winelands of **Montepulciano** and **Montalcino**. There are tips throughout, from seeking out what's free to avoiding the crowds, plus ten easy-to-follow itineraries that tie together a clutch of sights in a short space of time. Add inspiring photography and easy-to-use maps, and you've got the essential pocket-sized travel companion to Florence and Tuscany. As the locals say, "Buon viaggio!" **Enjoy the book, and enjoy Florence and Tuscany.**

Clockwise from top: Sorano, Pisa's Leaning Tower, the Tuscan countryside, Florence's Ponte Vecchio, Michelangelo's *David*, Viareggio's Carnevale, Montepulciano's Palazzo Bucelli.

Exploring Florence and Tuscany

With its world-famous art cities, exquisite medieval hill towns and iconic vine- and olive-clad hills, Tuscany has so much to see that it can be difficult to decide where to start. These itineraries are designed to make planning your trip easy, concentrating on the places that no one should miss.

Key

━ Two-day itinerary
━ Seven-day itinerary

Florence's Ponte Vecchio still has shops on it, as was common in the Middle Ages.

Two Days in Florence

Day ❶

MORNING

Begin with the splendid **Duomo Group** *(see pp16–17)*. Climb to the top of the Campanile then admire the Gothic Baptistry. Walk to **Piazza della Signoria** *(see p83)*, which is overlooked by **Palazzo Vecchio** *(see p83)*, then cross the Arno via the medieval **Ponte Vecchio** *(see p82)* with its minuscule jewellery shops.

AFTERNOON

Visit the **Pitti Palace** *(see pp18–21)* for Raphael's *La Velata* then stroll around the **Boboli Gardens** *(see p18)*. End the day at the **Uffizi** *(see pp12–15)*, being sure to admire Botticelli's *La Primavera* and *Birth of Venus*.

Day ❷

MORNING

Head to **Santa Croce** *(see p82)*, where the Cappella de' Pazzi is an icon of Renaissance architecture, then move on to **Il Bargello** *(see p82)*, which houses sculptures including *Flying Mercury* by Giambologna. Devote the rest of the morning to Fra Angelico's frescoes at **San Marco** *(see p82)*.

AFTERNOON

Pay homage to Michelangelo's *David* at the **Galleria dell'Accademia** *(see p81)*. Afterwards, look at scenes from the New Testament by Ghirlandaio in the church of **Santa Maria Novella** *(see p56)*. Take bus 12 from the train station to **San Miniato al Monte** *(see p57)*, for splendid views and a marble medieval horoscope.

The beautiful Tuscan countryside is dotted with iconic cypress trees.

Seven Days in Tuscany

Days ❶ and ❷
Follow the two-day Florence itinerary.

Day ❸
Arrive in **Pisa** *(see pp26–9)* and make a beeline for the Campo dei Miracoli, dominated by the Leaning Tower. Next, visit the market on arcaded Piazza Vettovaglie and then stroll along the languid Arno before driving to **Lucca** *(see pp46–7)*.

Day ❹
Begin at Lucca's Duomo, housing the *Volto Santo*. Next, walk around the town's ramparts before heading to the Piazza del Mercato, which retains the form of the Roman amphitheatre that preceded it. Then drive south to **San Gimignano** *(see pp24–5)*, for its medieval towers and formidably crenellated private and civic buildings. Visit the Collegiata with its 14th-century frescoes by Bartolo di Fredi. Pick up an ice cream at Piazza della Cisterna's Gelateria "di Piazza" (Gelateria Dondoli).

Day ❺
Tour the **Chianti Classico** wine region *(see pp38–41)*, stopping for tasters along the way. From Panzano a minor road leads to the picturesque wine hamlet of Volpaia, close to Radda in Chianti. Afterwards, head through the scenic Tuscan countryside to **Siena** *(see pp30–37)*.

Day ❻
Explore Piazza del Campo and visit the medieval art collection of the Palazzo Pubblico. Climb the Torre del Mangia, before heading to the striped Duomo. In the evening, drive to **Cortona** *(see pp42–5)*.

Day ❼
Spend the morning exploring Cortona, with its Etruscan museum and tombs and medieval alleyways. Be sure to visit the Museo Diocesano for Fra Angelico's *Annunciation* before driving back to Florence.

San Gimignano, with its imposing medieval towers, is one of Tuscany's most evocative hill towns.

0 km   30
0 miles   30

Top 10 Florence and Tuscany Highlights

Marble façade and campanile of the Duomo

TOP 10 Florence and Tuscany Highlights

Limiting the choice of prime sights to ten is not an easy task in a land as rich and varied as Tuscany. Its storybook landscape is home to medieval hill towns, fabled wines and an unrivalled collection of Renaissance artistic masterpieces. Here are the best of the best.

The Uffizi, Florence ①

A veritable who's who of the greatest Renaissance masters is installed in the former *uffizi* ("offices") of Florence's ruling Medici family (see pp12–15).

The Duomo Group, Florence ②

Brunelleschi's noble dome, Giotto's slender bell tower, Ghiberti's robust gates, Michelangelo's tortured *Pietà* and two panoramic terraces, all wrapped in red, white and green marble, are a magnificent sight (see pp16–17).

Pitti Palace, Florence ③

This massive Medici palace has a painting collection to rival the Uffizi, with porcelain, silver, carriages and modern art on display, as well as formal gardens (see pp18–21).

San Gimignano ④

A medieval fairy-tale town with stone towers and frescoed churches, surrounded by patchwork fields and terraced vineyards (see pp24–5).

Pontremoli

Aulla

Alpi Apuane

Massa

Bagni di Lucca

Pietrasanta

Pist

Viareggio

⑩ Lucca

Pisa ⑤

Arno

Ponted

Ponsac

Livorno

Rosignano Solvay

Volterra

Cecina

Ligurian Sea

Larderell

San Vincenzo

Venturina Terme

Piombino

Foll

Portoferraio

Isola d'Elba

| 0 km | 30 |
| 0 miles | 30 |

5 Campo dei Miracoli, Pisa
A grassy "Field of Miracles", the Campo is studded with masterpieces of Romanesque architecture: the Baptistry and Duomo containing Gothic pulpits by the Pisanos and, of course, that famous leaning bell tower (see pp26–9).

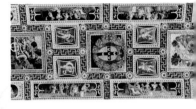

6 Siena's Duomo
A striped giant of a cathedral, the Duomo is stuffed with carvings, frescoes, Michelangelo's sculptures and Bernini's chapel (see pp30–33).

7 Siena's Campo and Palazzo Pubblico
This lovely brick square is Siena's living room, its graceful Palazzo Pubblico a museum celebrating the maestros of Gothic art (see pp34–7).

8 Chianti
The ultimate Tuscan idyll, this is a landscape of steeply rolling hills clad in rows of grapevines, topped by castles and dotted with countryside *trattorie* serving up Italy's most famous wine (see pp38–41).

9 Cortona
This is Tuscany in miniature: medieval atmosphere, great art, handcrafted ceramics, sweeping views and fine wines (see pp42–5).

Lucca 10
Medieval towers and 16th-century ramparts have been domesticated as small parks in this elegant city of Romanesque façades and opera (see pp46–7).

TOP 10 ⭐ The Uffizi, Florence

This museum is the ultimate Renaissance primer, from Giotto, Botticelli, Leonardo da Vinci and Michelangelo to Raphael, Titian, Caravaggio and beyond. This historic progression is only fitting, as the building, originally the *uffizi* ("offices") of the ruling Medici family, was designed by Giorgio Vasari, who wrote the world's first art history text. Some 1,700 works are on display, with another 1,400 in storage. These galleries shelter an abundance of masterpieces that demand a visit of at least three or four hours.

5 The Annunciation

One of the earliest works (1475) of that versatile master Leonardo da Vinci. His attention to detail is already apparent in the flower-bedecked lawn and the drapery. Leonardo's patented *sfumato* style creates the illusion of great distance by introducing a hazy atmosphere.

6 Maestà

Giotto's *Maestà* of 1310 is revolutionary compared with nearby similar scenes by his older contemporaries Duccio and Cimabue. Here, the Madonna has bulk beneath her clothing, and depth is created through the placing of the surrounding figures on solid ground **(below)**.

1 Birth of Venus

Botticelli's Venus on a shell (c.1484–6) is the ultimate Renaissance beauty **(above)**. While the pose is classical, the face is said to be Simonetta Vespucci's, the girlfriend of Piero de' Medici, and cousin to the explorer Amerigo Vespucci.

3 Tondo Doni

A rare panel painting (1504) by Michelangelo, the *Tondo Doni* or *Holy Family* owes much to Signorelli, but its twisting figures, exotic saturated colours and lounging nudes predict Mannerism.

2 Madonna with Child and Two Angels

This painting (c.1565) by Filippo Lippi is one of the most admired of the Renaissance. Its composition would become a model for many painters, such as Botticelli. The landscape is inspired by Flemish paintings.

4 La Primavera

Botticelli's companion work to his *Birth of Venus*, *La Primavera* (1478) is populated by goddesses and over 500 species of plant. The painting's exact meaning is not known but it may be a Neoplatonic allegory of spring based around a poem by Poliziano.

7 Federico da Montefeltro and Battista Sforza

Piero della Francesca's intense, psychological style of portraiture unflinchingly depicts his patrons, the Duke and Duchess of Urbino, warts and all **(left)**.

MUSEUM GUIDE

Coming from the Piazza della Signoria, enter on the left (east) side of the U-shaped loggia; one entrance is for reserved tickets and Firenze Card-holders, the other for walk-ins. The top-floor galleries line a long corridor, rooms 2–24 in the east wing, 25–45 in the west. The newer Sale Blu, Rosse and Gialle (Blue, Red and Yellow Rooms) downstairs double back towards the shop next to the entrance/exit.

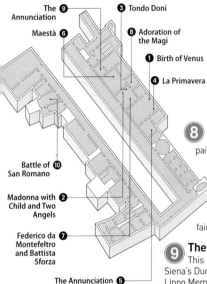

The Annunciation ❾
Maestà ❻
❸ Tondo Doni
❽ Adoration of the Magi
❶ Birth of Venus
❹ La Primavera
Battle of San Romano ❿
Madonna with Child and Two Angels ❷
Federico da Montefeltro and Battista Sforza ❼
The Annunciation ❺

8 Adoration of the Magi

This large work (1423), painted in tempera on wood by Gentile da Fabriano, is one of the masterpieces of the International Gothic style, with its sumptuous colours, depiction of elegant clothes and a fairy-tale atmosphere.

9 The Annunciation

This 1333 panel was painted for Siena's Duomo by Simone Martini and Lippo Memmi. The Virgin's expression – almost surprise or fear – gives the work a great sense of reality. The delicate, elegant lines and colours make this a Sienese Gothic masterpiece.

10 Battle of San Romano

A master of perspective, Uccello experimented with it to the detriment of the scene. The lances in this third of his 1456 masterpiece (the other pieces are in Paris and London) over-define a perspective plane, while the background tilts at a radical angle **(above)**.

NEED TO KNOW

MAP M–N4 ▪ Piazzale degli Uffizi 6 (off Piazza della Signoria) ▪ 055 294 883 (reservations) ▪ www.uffizi.it

Open 8:15am–6:50pm Tue–Sun (last entry 45 min before closing); closed 1 Jan, 1 May, 25 Dec

Adm

▪ Take a break at the outdoor café at the end of the west wing galleries, above the Loggia de' Lanzi.

▪ The queue to enter can last hours. Booking ahead or online in order to jump the queue is worth the small fee.

▪ The Uffizi is undergoing major expansion and exhibits are likely to change location. Inquire at the gallery or check online for an update.

The Uffizi Collections

Masaccio's *Sant'Anna Metterza*

1 Early Renaissance
(Rooms 7–9)

The earthiness of Masaccio and the delicacy of Fra Angelico join the likes of Paolo Uccello in Room 7. Renaissance ideals develop further with anatomically exacting works by the Pollaiuolo brothers and the flowing lines of Masaccio's more elegant student Filippo Lippi, whose *Madonna with Child and Two Angels* is also here *(see p12)*. These lead up to the languid grace of Lippi's protégé, Botticelli.

2 Botticelli
(Rooms 10–14)

Tear your eyes away from the famed *Birth of Venus* and *La Primavera (see p12)* to admire other Botticelli master-pieces such as *Pallas and the Centaur* and his *Adoration of the Magi* featuring a self-portrait (in yellow robes on the right).

Michelangelo's *Tondo Doni*

Compare this *Adoration* with those by Botticelli's student, Filippino Lippi, and by Botticelli's contemporary (and Michelangelo's teacher), Ghirlandaio.

3 Pre-Renaissance
(Rooms 2–6)

The first Uffizi room bridges the medieval and proto-Renaissance with a trio of *Maestàs*, from Cimabue's Byzantine work through Duccio's Sienese Gothic style to Giotto's version *(see p12)*. Simone Martini's *Annunciation (see p13)* represents the graceful 14th-century Sienese School. Gentile da Fabriano and Lorenzo Monaco give one final, colourful shout of the medieval in the International Gothic style of the early 15th century.

4 Leonardo da Vinci
(Rooms 15 and 79)

Rooms 15 and 79 celebrate Verrocchio's star pupils, including Lorenzo di Credi, Botticini, Umbrian master Perugino (Raphael's teacher) and Leonardo da Vinci himself. As an apprentice, Leonardo painted the angel on the left of Verrocchio's *Baptism of Christ*. Leonardo da Vinci's restored *Annunciation (see p12)* and his unfinished, chaotic *Adoration of the Magi* round out the room.

5 High Renaissance and Mannerism
(Room 35, Sale Rosse)

After some Peruginos, Signorellis and a Venetian interlude, Room 35 marks the start of the High Renaissance, with Michelangelo's *Tondo Doni*. Andrea del Sarto and his students developed the colours and asymmetrical posi-tioning of Michelangelo into Mannerism. Later in the Sale Rosse are

Bronzino's iconic Medici portraits and precise compositions by Raphael and Titian.

6 European Masters
(Rooms 47–50 in the Sale Blu)

Opened in 2011, the Sale Blu display is part of the Uffizi's vast collection of non-Italian works, in rooms that were severely damaged by a bomb in 1993. The display includes significant 16th- to 18th-century Spanish works by Goya, El Greco and Velázquez. Portraits by Rembrandt van Rijn and works by Rubens also hang here. Sale Blu and Rooms 90–93 (below) are on the first floor and hence not shown on the floorplan.

7 Baroque
(Rooms 90–93 in the Sale Gialle)

The Uffizi's post-Renaissance collections are not outstanding, save for a few works by Caravaggio – a *Sacrifice of Isaac*, *Medusa* and *Bacchus*. The last is typical of Caravaggio's realistic style. He depicts the deity as a common man, of the sort he might have come across in a tavern. Of his followers,

so-called *caravaggeschi* works include *Judith and Holofernes* by Artemisia Gentileschi, the first woman to become a member of the Accademia delle Arti del Disegno.

8 The Tribune (Room 18)

The Uffizi's original display space is a room decorated with mother-of-pearl and inlaid *pietre dure*, built by Francesco I to show off the *Medici Venus* and other classical statues. Portraits by Bronzino and Pontormo, Rosso Fiorentino's lute-plucking *Musician Angel* and Raphael's *St John in the Desert* cover the walls.

9 U-Shaped Corridor

The second-floor main corridor linking the galleries is lined with statues. These are mostly Roman copies of Greek originals **(left)**. Its ceiling vaults are frescoed (1581) with grotesques depicting Florence's history, leaders, thinkers and artists. The views from the short south corridor are celebrated.

Boy with Thorn, U-Shaped Corridor

10 Vasari Corridor

The 1-km (0.6-mile) corridor between the Pitti Palace and the Palazzo Vecchio, passing through the Uffizi, was damaged during a 1993 terrorist bombing. Lined with works from the 17th to 20th centuries, it is open only for prebooked tours: contact Firenze Musei or go to www.florenceandtuscanytours.com.

Bacchus by Caravaggio

Plan of the Uffizi

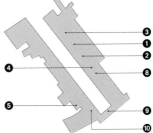

TOP 10 ⭐ The Duomo Group, Florence

Florence's gorgeous cathedral offers two panoramic views, one atop Giotto's lithe and lovely bell tower, the other at the summit of Brunelleschi's robust and noble dome. The interior of the cathedral contains some Uccello frescoes but otherwise is oddly barren and less interesting than clambering up between the layers of the dome. The nearby Baptistry is also more rewarding with its glinting Byzantine mosaics and *Gates of Paradise,* while inside the museum are statues by Michelangelo, Donatello, Ghirlandaio and Pisano.

Duomo: Dome ③

The crossing of the Duomo was thought unspannable until 1420 when Brunelleschi came up with an ingenious double shell solution **(right)**. Forget the dull frescoes inside; the thrill is to climb between the layers to the marble lantern at its peak.

① Baptistry: Gates of Paradise

Lorenzo Ghiberti's gilded bronze panels (1425–52) showcase his mastery at depicting great depth in shallow relief **(above)**. Michelangelo was reportedly so moved he proclaimed they would "grace the very gates of Paradise", and the name stuck. The original doors are housed in the Museo dell'Opera del Duomo.

② Duomo: New Sacristy

The bronze doors and glazed terracotta lunette are 15th-century works by Luca della Robbia. The interior, sheathed in wood inlay, was where Lorenzo de' Medici took refuge after an assassination attempt in 1478.

④ Duomo: Fresco of Giovanni Acuto

Master of perspective, Paolo Uccello painted this trompe l'oeil fresco (1436) of an equestrian statue as a memorial for John Hawkwood, an English *condottiero* (mercenary leader) long in Florence's employ.

⑤ Duomo: Campanile

Giotto designed only the lowest level of the "Lily of Florence" **(left)**, which was continued by Andrea Pisano and finished by Francesco Talenti. It is 85 m (276 ft), or 414 steps, to the top.

6 Baptistry: Mosaics

The glittering swathe of 13th-century mosaic panels tells stories from Genesis and the lives of Jesus, Joseph and St John the Baptist (above).

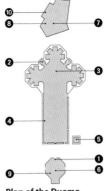

Plan of the Duomo

8 Museo dell'Opera del Duomo: Habakkuk

One of several prophets Donatello carved for the Campanile, this one was nicknamed *Lo Zuccone* – "Pumpkinhead" – by irreverent Florentines.

9 Baptistry: North Doors

Lorenzo Ghiberti won the 1401 competition to cast these 28 bronze panels, and spent 21 years creating what art historians consider the first proper Renaissance work.

10 Museo dell'Opera: Michelangelo's Pietà

Michelangelo created three *Pietàs*; the second of these (below) in 1548–55, which he later attacked in frustration.

7 Museo dell'Opera del Duomo: Altar Front

This ornate silver and gilt scene for the Baptistry took Verrocchio, Antonio Pollaiuolo, Michelozzo and other sculptors over 100 years to craft, from 1366 to 1480.

DUOMO HISTORY

Florence's Baptistry was probably founded in the 6th century, but its structure is mostly 11th- to 14th-century. The massive cathedral itself wasn't started until 1294, when Arnolfo di Cambio began building around the diminutive old Santa Reparata; it was largely finished by 1417. Brunelleschi's engineering added the dome in 1436, which was topped in the 1460s by Verrocchio's bronze. The Neo-Gothic façade is 19th-century.

NEED TO KNOW

MAP M–N3 ▪ Piazza del Duomo

Duomo: open 10am–5pm Mon–Fri, 10am–3pm Sat, 1:30–4:45pm Sun

Dome: open 8:30am–7pm Mon–Fri, to 5pm Sat, 1–4pm Sun

Baptistry: open 8:15–10:15am & 1:15–7:30pm Mon–Fri, 8:15am–6.30pm Sat, 8:15am–1:30pm Sun

Campanile: open 8:15am–7pm daily

Museum: open 9am–6:50pm daily

Adm: the €15 combined ticket is valid for 48 hours from first usage

▪ I Fratellini (*see p86*) is a tiny hole-in-the-wall place serving glasses of wine and sandwiches to customers who eat standing out on the cobblestoned street.

▪ The last ascent of the dome is 40 minutes before closing; queue early in summertime.

TOP 10 ⭐ Pitti Palace, Florence

This one-time residence of the Medici family is a treasure-trove: there are royal apartments, galleries of modern art, costume, silverware and porcelain. Above all, there is the Galleria Palatina, frescoed by Pietro da Cortona, and second only to the Uffizi. It contains one of the world's best collections of Raphaels and Titians. The paintings are still hung 19th-century style, when "Does that Tintoretto match the room's decor?" or "Let's put all the round ones together" mattered more than any didactic arrangement.

2 La Velata

Raphael did many portraits, usually of Madonnas, and several of his best are in these collections. *La Velata* (1516) is his masterpiece of portraiture, displaying his mastery of colour, light and form (left). The sitter is most likely La Fornarina, his Roman girlfriend *(see p20)*.

3 Consequences of War

Venus tries to stop Mars going to war, while Fate encourages him *(see p21)*. This was Rubens's plea against his country becoming embroiled in the Thirty Years' War.

The Pitti Palace

1 Mary Magdalene

This is the first (1535) of many Mary Magdalenes painted by the Venetian master Titian *(see p20)*.

4 Boboli Gardens

The Renaissance garden with Baroque and Rococo touches has cypress avenues, hidden statues and burbling fountains.

5 Three Ages of Man

The attribution of this allegorical work (1500) to Giorgione is not certain, but it is a beautiful piece with strong colour and composition *(see p20)*. Compare it to Pietro da Cortona's Baroque *Four Ages of Man* (1637), frescoed on the ceiling of the Sala della Stufa *(see p21)*.

6 Madonna and Child

In a masterful touch, Filippo Lippi placed the Madonna's chin in the geometric centre of this work (below), helping to unite a complex composition involving both the main scene and background images from the Virgin's life *(see p21)*.

MUSEUM GUIDE

Enter via Ammannati's Courtyard (the ticket office is to the right of Pitti Palace). Galleria Palatina and the royal apartments are on the first floor, but see the Palatina first. The Boboli entrance is in the back right-hand corner. The other collections are: Modern Art Gallery; Costume Gallery (in the Meridiana Summer Palace); Silver Collection (ground floor); Porcelain Museum (at the top of the Boboli); Carriage Museum (left wing, but currently closed).

7 Grotta Grande

This Mannerist cavern **(above)** is dripping with stylized stalactites, Giambologna statues and plaster casts of Michelangelo's *Slaves*.

10 Green Room, the Royal Apartments

The best-preserved room in the *Appartamenti Reali* contains such lavish furnishings as an ebony cabinet inlaid with semiprecious stones and bronze. The ceiling of the Green Room is decorated with trompe l'oeil stuccoes and a canvas by Luca Giordano.

8 Ammannati's Courtyard

Mannerist architecture was a robust, oversized take on the Renaissance. Bartolomeo Ammannati expounded this in dramatic, heavily rusticated Classical orders in this *cortile* (1560–70).

9 The Tuscan Maremma

On the second floor (not shown on the floorplan), the modern art gallery's jewel is Giovanni Fattori's 1850 work. He was the best of the Macchiaioli, a 19th-century Tuscan school with parallels with Impressionism.

NEED TO KNOW

MAP L5 ▪ Piazza de' Pitti ▪ 055 294 883 (Galleria Palatina and Appartamenti Reali)

Galleria Palatina and Appartamenti Reali: open 8:15am–6:50pm Tue–Sun, closed 1 Jan, 1 May & 25 Dec

Galleria del Costume: open 8:15am–6:50pm, closed Mon, 1 Jan, 1 May & 25 Dec

Museo della Porcellana, Museo degli Argenti and Boboli Gardens: open Nov–Feb: 8:15am–4:30pm; Mar to 5:30pm; Apr, May, Sep & Oct to 6:30pm; Jun–Aug to 7.30pm daily; closed 1st & last Mon of the month, 1 Jan, 1 May & 25 Dec

Adm (Uffizi, Boboli and Pitti combined ticket available Mar–Oct)

▪ Pitti Gola e Cantina, just across the piazza, offers light meals and snacks *(see p86)*.

▪ Officially picnics are not allowed in the Boboli Gardens.

▪ If you liked the Pitti Palace's beautiful *pietre dure* table *(see p21)*, buy yourself a modern version at Pitti Mosaici on the Piazza de' Pitti.

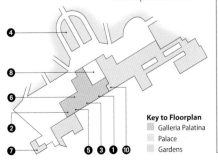

4
8
6
2
7

5 3 1 10

Key to Floorplan
▨ Galleria Palatina
▢ Palace
▨ Gardens

Pitti Palace: Galleria Palatina

Giorgione's *Three Ages of Man*

1 Sala di Giove

This room holds two of Pitti's top sights: Raphael's *La Velata* and Giorgione's *Three Ages of Man* (see p18). Early Renaissance master-pieces include Perugino's *Madonna del Sacco*, a subtle study of spatial relationships, and a small, wrinkly *St Jerome* either by Verrocchio or Piero di Pollaiuolo. Andrea del Sarto painted *St John the Baptist* (1523) in a classical style, but his *Annunciation* (1512) is proto-Mannerist. Fra Bartolomeo's *Lamentation of the Dead Christ* (1512) and Bronzino's *Guidobaldo Della Rovere* (1532) are High Renaissance works that anticipate the Baroque.

2 Sala di Saturno

Raphael's entire career is covered here, from the Leonardesque *Madonna del Granduca* (1506) to his late *Vision of Ezekiel* (1518). Among his other Madonnas and portraits, seek out the Mona Lisa-inspired *Maddalena Doni* (1506), which heavily influenced Renaissance portraiture. Raphael's teacher Perugino painted a strikingly composed *Lamentation of the Dead Christ* (1495). Fra Bartolomeo's *Stupor Mundi* (1516) and del Sarto's *Annunciation and Dispute of the Trinity* (1517) round out the room.

3 Sala di Apollo

Titian finds a home here: his *Mary Magdalene* (see p18) hangs near his *Portrait of an Englishman* (1540). Influential works abound: Andrea del Sarto's *Pietà* (1522) and *Holy Family* (1523) helped found the Mannerist style. The tight, focused power of the *Sacred Conversation* (1522), by del Sarto's student Rosso Fiorentino, was affected when the painting was later artificially extended to fit a large Baroque frame. The classical style of Bolognese artists Guido Reni (a late *Cleopatra*) and Guercino (an early *Resurrection of Tabitha*) helped inform the burgeoning Baroque.

4 Sala di Venere

The centrepiece of the room is a *Venus* carved by Canova to replace the ancient original Napoleon had shipped back to Paris (it is now in the Uffizi). Titian steals the show with *The Concert* (1510; Giorgione may also have contributed), a *Portrait of Julius II* (1545) copied from Raphael and the celebrated *Portrait of Pietro Aretino* (1545). Rubens's bucolic work *Return from the Hayfields* is often overlooked.

5 Sala dell'Educazione di Giove

There are two works of particular note in this room: Caravaggio's *Sleeping Cupid* (1608) is a study in realism and chiaroscuro. Cristofano Allori's *Judith Beheading Holofernes* has double meanings: every face in it is a portrait from life. Judith is the artist's girlfriend, the old woman looking on bears the face of her mother and the decapitated head of Holofernes is Cristofano Allori's self-portrait.

***Venus*, Sala di Venere**

6 Later Works

Some of the rest can't live up to the highlights, though the names – Tintoretto, Rubens, Botticelli, Pontormo – remain major. The only masterworks are Raphael's *Madonna dell'Impannata* (1514) and a 1450 Filippo Lippi *Madonna and Child (see p18)*, the museum's oldest painting. Compare Signorelli's *Sacra Famiglia*, which influenced Michelangelo's in the Uffizi, with that of Beccafumi – a Mannerist take informed by the work of Michelangelo.

7 Sala dell'Iliade

Raphael's unusual, almost Flemish-style portrait of a pregnant woman, *La Gravida* (1506), is the star of the room. Andrea del Sarto is represented by a pair of *Assumptions* (painted 1523 and 1526). Artemisia Gentileschi is also represented: she was the Baroque's only noted female artist *(see p15)* and often portrayed strong female biblical characters, including Mary Magdalene and Judith, in her works.

8 Sala di Marte

Rubens dominates with the 1638 *Consequences of War (see p18)* and *Four Philosophers* (1612), which includes portraits of himself (far left) and his brother. The fine collection includes the penetrating *Portrait of a Man* (1550), which is attributed to

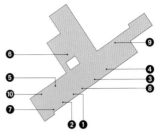

Plan of the Galleria Palatina

Paolo Veronese, *Luigi Cornaro* (1560), which is now attributed to Tintoretto, *Ippolito de' Medici* (1532) by Titian and *Cardinal Bentivoglio* by Van Dyck.

9 Galleria delle Statue

Paintings are on temporary display in this long entrance hall, but a few have been here for years, including Caravaggio's violent genre scene *The Toothpuller* (officially an Uffizi painting) and an early Rubens *Risen Christ*. Don't miss the 19th-century table which is a fine example of *pietre dure*, the art of inlaid stone.

10 Sala della Stufa and Napoleon's Bathroom

The Sala della Stufa preserves Pietro da Cortona frescoes and 1640 majolica flooring. Napoleon's Empire-style bathroom is one of the few Pitti Palace remnants of the Frenchman's brief Italian reign.

Consequences of War by Rubens in the Sala di Marte

🔟 ⭐ San Gimignano

Souvenir shops notwithstanding, this pedestrianized hill town is the most evocative of the Middle Ages of any in Tuscany. This UNESCO World Heritage Site is nicknamed San Gimignano delle Belle Torri, or San Gimignano of the Beautiful Towers. More than 70 of these towers once attested to this medieval Manhattan's wealth; 14 still spike its skyline today. The town boasts, for its size, a wealth of 14th- and 15th-century art. Modern art, too, is tucked into unexpected corners, and there is an excellent local white wine.

① Collegiata

The plain exterior belies an interior covered in frescoes **(below)**. The ones on the right wall are by Lippo Memmi (1333–41), those on the left by Bartolo di Fredi (1367). Taddeo di Bartolo painted the gory *Last Judgement* (1410) in the nave and Benozzo Gozzoli created *St Sebastian* (1464) at the entrance. The town's pride are the Domenico Ghirlandaio frescoes (1475) in the Chapel of Santa Fina.

The atmospheric hill town of San Gimignano

③ Museo Civico

San Gimignano's best museum is situated on the first floor of the Palazzo del Popolo, beneath the lofty Torre Grossa. The collection includes the 1511 work *Madonna with Saints Gregory and Benedict* by Pinturicchio, a *Maestà* by Lippo Memmi and works by Filippino Lippi and Benozzo Gozzoli. Memmo di Filuppucci's 14th-century frescoes depicting a couple's marriage and their wedding night are unusually erotic for the period.

② Torre Grossa

You can climb all 54 m (175 ft) of the tallest tower in town for one of Italy's most stupendous views, across the surrounding towers and terracotta roofs to the rolling hills all around.

Museo della Tortura ④

A grisly array of torture instruments occupies the Torre della Diavola or She-Devil's Tower **(right)**. The explanatory placards make for grim reading, pointing out which of the devices are still used around the world today.

Previous pages View from Torre del Mangia, Siena

5 Façade of San Francesco

The Romanesque façade of a long-vanished church remains wedged between later medieval buildings. Behind it is a local vineyard's *cantina*, offering wine tastings and, beyond, a pretty, shaded terrace with fine country views.

6 Sant'Agostino

Most tourists miss this little church **(right)** with its 1483 Piero di Pollaiuolo altarpiece and Gozzoli's quirky, colourful apse frescoes on the life of St Augustine (1465). Benedetto da Maiano carved the tomb of San Bartolo (1488) against the west wall.

7 Museo d'Arte Sacra

This modest museum of liturgical art stands on a pretty piazza off the left flank of the Collegiata. Highlights of the collection are a *Madonna and Child* by Bartolo di Fredi and 14th-century illuminated choir books.

8 Rocca

The 14th-century fortress has long since crumbled to a romantic ruin, and is now planted with olive and fig trees. Scramble up its ramparts to get a picture-perfect view of the town's tall towers.

SAN GIMIGNANO'S HISTORY

The Etruscan and later Roman settlement blossomed as a way-point on the medieval Via Francigena pilgrim route. Competing local families built the towers as a competitive display of wealth as well as for defence. A devastating plague in 1348 left the town under Florentine control, and the pilgrim route shifted east. San Gimignano gradually became a backwater, its medieval character preserved to this day.

9 Museo Archeologico

The small collection of Etruscan artifacts here includes a curious funerary urn topped by a reclining effigy of the deceased, his cup holding a coin to pay for entry into the afterlife.

10 Piazza della Cisterna

This triangular piazza **(below)**, ringed with 13th- and 14th-century towers and centred on a 1237 stone well, will be familiar as a setting for such films as *Where Angels Fear to Tread* and *Tea with Mussolini*.

NEED TO KNOW

MAP D3 ■ Tourist office on Piazza del Duomo 1 ■ 0577 940 008 ■ www.sangimignano.com

Collegiata: open daily (closed 16–31 Jan & 16–30 Nov). Adm: €4

Museo Civico: open daily. Adm: €9

Museo della Tortura: open daily. Adm: €10

Museo Archeologico: open daily. Adm: combined ticket with Museo Civico

Museo d'Arte Sacra: open daily Mar–Dec. Adm: €3.50

Combined tickets are available from the tourist office

■ Gelateria "di Piazza" *(see p118)* serves the best gelato in town.

■ Spend the night to enjoy the town like a local after the tour buses leave.

TOP 10 ⭐ Campo dei Miracoli, Pisa

Pisa's "Field of Miracles", a UNESCO World Heritage Site, is one of Italy's most gorgeous squares, its green carpet of grass the setting for the Pisan-Romanesque gemstones of the Duomo, Camposanto, Baptistry and Campanile – that icon better known as the Leaning Tower. The east end of the square is anchored by the old bishop's palace, now the Duomo museum. Souvenir stalls cling like barnacles to the square's south side; a doorway between them opens into the Museo delle Sinopie, housing the giant preparatory sketches on plaster for the lost Camposanto frescoes.

3 Leaning Tower

This bell tower in the Pisan-Romanesque style was begun in 1173 and started leaning when builders were only on the third level **(left)**. By 1990, the tower was 4.5 m (15 ft) out of vertical, and was closed for engineers to reverse the tilt. They announced in 2008 that it had been stabilized.

4 Duomo Façade

A triumph of blind arcades, stacked open arches and coloured marble decorations **(right)**. Giambologna cast the bronze doors to replace those destroyed by fire in 1595.

1 Duomo's San Ranieri Doors

Buscheto sculpted in 1180 the only remaining Romanesque bronze doors of Pisa's cathedral, gracing them with minimalist biblical scenes and palm trees. The original doors are now in the Museo dell'Opera.

5 Museo delle Sinopie

Restorers discovered sketches for the lost Camposanto frescoes, offering an insight into the creative process of these medieval artists.

2 Duomo Pulpit

Nicola Pisano's son, Giovanni, carved this in 1302–11 **(right)**. The Gothic naturalism of its tumultuous New Testament scenes probably reflects the influence of Giotto, who was a contemporary working in Padua.

ORIENTATION

The Campo dei Miracoli is a 15- to 20-minute bus ride from Pisa Centrale station (take No. 4 or the LAM Rossa) or a 15-minute walk from Pisa San Rossore station. Admission to the sites is available in several configurations; currently these are as follows: a free ticket for the Duomo alone; €5 for any one site, €7 for two, €8 for three except the Tower; €18 for the Tower alone. The city walls are also accessed for free.

6 Museo dell'Opera del Duomo

This rich collection includes an 11th-century Islamic bronze hippogriff (half horse, half griffin). Taken in a Crusade, this once topped the cathedral dome. Currently closed for renovation.

Plan of the Campo dei Miracoli

7 Baptistry

Italy's largest Baptistry started life as a Romanesque piece (1153) but has a Gothic dome. The acoustically perfect interior houses a great Gothic pulpit by sculptor Nicola Pisano.

8 Baptistry Pulpit

Nicola Pisano's Gothic masterpiece (1255–60) depicts a number of religious scenes based on ancient pagan reliefs decorating the sarcophagi in the Camposanto.

9 Camposanto

This former cemetery, which contains recycled Roman sarcophagi, once boasted frescoes to rival those in the Sistine Chapel, such as this one by Buffalmacco (below). Although largely destroyed in World War II, a few sections are preserved in a back room.

NEED TO KNOW

MAP C3 ▪ Tourist office: Piazza del Duomo 7; 050 560 464 ▪ Campo dei Miracoli: 050 550 100; www.opapisa.it

Duomo: open daily. Adm: free, though a pass from the ticket office is required

Tower: open daily. Adm: €18

Baptistry: open daily. Adm: €5

Camposanto: open daily. Adm: €5

Museo del Duomo: temporarily closed.

Museo delle Sinopie: open daily. Adm: €5

▪ Il Canguro (Via Santa Maria 151) has great sandwiches – head here for a quick and tasty lunch break.

▪ The opening times of sites vary; check online or with the tourist office.

10 Camposanto Triumph of Death Fresco

This fresco by Buffalmacco is the best of those that survived World War II. Its scene of Death riding across an apocalyptic landscape inspired Liszt to compose his *Totentanz* concerto.

Other Pisan Sights

① Museo San Matteo

Often-overlooked collection of 13th-century Crucifixions and such notable works as Simone Martini's *Virgin and Child with Saints* (1321), Nino Pisano's *Madonna del Latte* and Donatello's bust of San Rossore. Masaccio, Fra Angelico, Gozzoli, Lorenzo di Credi and Ghirlandaio are also represented.

② Santa Maria della Spina

The church is a pinnacled jewel of Gothic architecture built in 1230–1323 by Nino and Giovanni Pisano to house a thorn said to be from Christ's crown, brought back by a Pisan Crusader.

Detail, Santa Caterina mosaic

③ Piazza Vettovaglie Market

This attractive arcaded piazza stands at the centre of Pisa's colourful, lively outdoor food market.

④ Piazza dei Cavalieri

The probable site of the ancient forum is ringed by Giorgio Vasari's *sgrafitto* façade on the Palazzo dei Cavalieri (1562), the Baroque Santo Stefano church and the Palazzo dell'Orologio. It was in the last's tower that Count Ugolino, immortalized by Dante and Shelley, was accused of treason in 1288 and locked away to starve with his sons.

⑤ Santa Caterina

Behind the 1330 Gothic façade hides Nino Pisano's *Annunciation* and his tomb of Simone Saltarelli (1342), as well as Francesco Triani's *Apotheosis of St Thomas Aquinas* (1350).

⑥ Le Navi Antiche di Pisa

Thirty Roman ships, dating from 100 BC to AD 400 and probably sunk by flash floods or storms, were discovered in 1998 during work on San Rossore station (which was the harbour area before the Arno silted up). The ships' cargo and everyday accoutrements are being displayed in the Medici Arsenale as they are excavated, and will eventually be joined by the ships themselves.

Piazza dei Cavalieri

Certosa di Calci monastery

7 Certosa di Calci

This Carthusian monastery, set 12 km (8 miles) east of town, dates to 1366 and boasts Baroque frescoed chapels and cloisters.

8 Tenuta di San Rossore

Boar, deer and waterfowl abound in this coastal wildlife reserve. The poet Shelley's body was washed ashore here in 1822 after his boat sank and he drowned in the Gulf of Spezia.

9 San Paolo a Ripa d'Arno

This venerable church (805 AD) has a 13th-century façade and the Romanesque chapel of Sant'Agata is set in the grassy park behind.

10 San Nicola

Donato Bramante's Vatican steps were inspired by the bell tower stairs of this 1,000-year-old church.

THE LEANING TOWER

Italy's most famous symbol once leaned a staggering 15 ft (4.5 m) out of plumb. The problem: 55 m (180 ft) of marble stacked atop watery, alluvial sand. A worrisome list developed soon after building started in 1173. Work stopped until 1275, when it was decided to curve the tower back as it rose. By 1990, with over a million tourists annually tramping up the tower, collapse seemed imminent. The tower was closed, with restraining bands strapped around it, lead weights stacked on one side and the base excavated to try to reverse the lean. It eventually reopened at the end of 2001 for accompanied visits only (30 people admitted every half hour). Engineers and experts predicted in 2008 that the tower should remain stable for at least another 200 years.

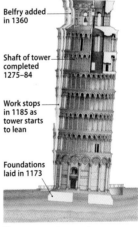

Belfry added in 1360

Shaft of tower completed 1275–84

Work stops in 1185 as tower starts to lean

Foundations laid in 1173

The tower rests on a stone platform. An attempt was made in 1836 to dig out the foundations, but the lean worsened so work stopped. Monitors placed in the soil below the foundations now track any movement.

CAMPO DEI MIRACOLI

VIA S. ZENO
VIA ROMA
VIA S. MARIA
VIA B. PISANNO
VIA S. FRANCESCO
Arno
LUNG MEDICEO
LUNG GALILEO
CORSO ITALIA
LUNG SONNINO
PIAZZA VITTORIO EMANUELE II

5 km (3 miles)

12 km (8 miles)

⑩⭐ Siena's Duomo

Siena's hulking Duomo is a treasure house of late Gothic sculpture, early Renaissance painting and Baroque design. Early architects dressed the edifice in striking Romanesque stripes, but its form is firmly Gothic, one of the best examples of the style in Italy. Equally fascinating are the Duomo's outbuildings: the Baptistry, the Museo dell'Opera Metropolitana and the Santa Maria della Scala hospital across the square, where 1440s frescoes in the wards depict medieval hospital scenes.

② Façade
Giovanni Pisano designed the façade **(left)** in 1285. His original time-worn statues (replaced now with copies) are in the Museo dell'Opera Metropolitana. The mosaics on the top half are by 19th-century Venetian craftsmen.

① Pisano Pulpit
Nicola Pisano's son, Giovanni, and his pupil Arnolfo di Cambio helped create this masterpiece of Gothic carving. Similar to Pisano pulpits in Pisa and Pistoia, it depicts scenes from the Life of Christ.

③ Piccolomini Altar
Andrea Bregno's 1480 marble altar incorporates a *Madonna and Child* (1397–1400) by Jacopo della Quercia and four small statues of saints (1501–4) by the young Michelangelo.

④ San Giovanni Chapel
Giovanni di Stefano's Renaissance baptismal chapel (1492) is decorated with Pinturicchio frescoes and a bronze *St John the Baptist* (1457) by an ageing Donatello.

DUOMO HISTORY

The Duomo was largely built between 1215 and 1263 by, among others, Nicola Pisano. His son Giovanni designed the façade. In 1339, work began on a huge new nave. The idea was to turn the Duomo we see today into merely the transept of the largest church in Christendom. This plan was thwarted by the Black Death in 1348, and the would-be façade is now a terrace, while the unfinished nave wall now houses the cathedral museum.

⑤ Floor Panels
All 59 panels are on show in early autumn (usually mid-August to October), but some are visible all year. Between 1372 and 1547, these exquisite marble mosaics **(left)** were created by Siena's top artists, including Pinturicchio and Matteo di Giovanni, whose *Massacre of the Innocents* is masterful.

6 Duccio's Stained-Glass Window

Italy's earliest stained glass (1288) decorates the round window in the apse. Designed by Siena's great early Gothic master Duccio di Boninsegna, it underwent a thorough cleaning in the 1990s. The original has now been placed in the cathedral museum, the Museo dell'Opera Metropolitana.

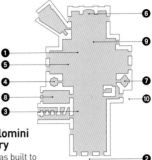

Plan of the Duomo

8 Piccolomini Library

The library was built to house manuscripts that belonged to the humanist Pope Pius II, born to Siena's Piccolomini family. His life is celebrated in masterly frescoes by Pinturicchio **(left)** that date from 1502 to 1507.

9 Choir

The intarsia wood choir stalls were made by various master craftsmen (1362–1570), the 1532 marble altar by Baldassarre Peruzzi, the angel candelabra (c.1488) by Francesco di Giorgio Martini and the apse *Ascension* fresco by Beccafumi from 1548 to 1551.

7 Chigi Chapel

Baroque master Gian Lorenzo Bernini designed this chapel in 1659. The 13th-century *Madonna del Volto* altarpiece is Siena's guardian angel: officials have placed the city keys before her in times of crisis, including during Nazi occupation, and Siena has always been delivered from harm.

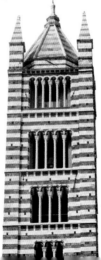

NEED TO KNOW

MAP E4 ▪ Piazza del Duomo 8 ▪ 0577 283 048 ▪ www.opera duomo.siena.it/en/

Duomo, library, crypt, museum, baptistry: 10:30am–7pm daily (to 5:30pm Nov–Feb)

Santa Maria della Scala: 10am–7pm (to 5pm Oct–Mar)

Adm: €4 for Duomo and library combined (Nov–Feb: Duomo free, €2 for the library), €7 when the floor is uncovered

▪ Nearby Bini is a traditional bakery that has been producing divine Sienese pastries since 1943 *(see p97)*.

▪ The floor panels are usually covered, but the preparatory drawings are on display at the Pinacoteca *(see p95)*.

▪ Several configurations of combined tickets exist – see the Duomo website for details.

10 Campanile

The tower **(left)** was added in 1313, but, with its dramatic black-and-white stripes, the design is Romanesque.

Sights on the Piazza del Duomo

Plan of the Piazza del Duomo

uses real arches to introduce trompe l'oeil painted ceiling vaults, creating a sense of deep space.

5 Santa Maria della Scala: Pellegrinaio

This ward in the former civic hospital features scenes painted in the 1440s by Domenico di Bartolo, including monks tending the sick. The symbolic orphans climbing a *scala* (ladder) to heaven are by Vecchietta.

6 Santa Maria della Scala: Museo Archeologico

The small but worthwhile collection includes Greek vases from Southern Italy, Etruscan bronzes and alabaster urns, and Roman coins.

1 Museo dell'Opera Metropolitana: Duccio's Maestà

The heavyweight masterpiece of Sienese Gothic painting. When Duccio finished it in 1311, Siena's citizens paraded it through the streets to the Duomo's altar.

7 Santa Maria della Scala: Fonte Gaia

The weathered remnants of Jacopo della Quercia's original Fonte Gaia sculptures (1409–19) have been removed from the Campo (see p34) to their own atmospheric gallery.

2 Museo dell'Opera Metropolitana: Madonna and Child

This is Donatello's *schiacciato* master-piece, combining an etched perspective background with dis-torted (when seen close up) high relief to create an illusion of depth in a nearly flat surface.

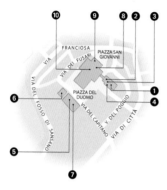

Madonna and Child

8 Baptistry: Ceiling Frescoes

Gaze heavenwards in the Baptistry and marvel at the dense frescoes by Vecchietta (1440s); note the inclu-sion of such delightful and whimsical details as a monstrous crocodile.

3 Museo dell'Opera Metropolitana: Panorama from the Façade

The museum inhabits what would have been the nave wall of the aborted expansion (see p30). Climb tight spiral stairs for great views.

9 Baptistry: Font

The brilliant bronze *Life of the Baptist* panels (1417–30) were cast by leading Florentine and Sienese sculptors that included Donatello and Ghiberti.

4 Museo dell'Opera Metropolitana: Birth of the Virgin

This richly coloured, highly detailed Gothic work by Pietro Lorenzetti

10 Duomo: Crypt

The frescoed chamber below the cathedral floor was only redis-covered in 2000. It is still uncertain who painted what, but everything dates to the late 1200s.

MIRACLES AND RELICS

The church of Santa Maria della Spina

Countless miracles have punctuated history in this fervently Christian land of saints and holy relics. When the crucifix in the church of Santa Trinita in Florence nodded its head in 1028 to Giovanni Gualberto, a local nobleman, he was moved to become a monk; he went on to found the Vallombrosan monastic order. The miraculous powers of the Madonna panel in a Florence granary and a Prato prison assured the buildings' transformations into the churches of Orsanmichele and Santa Maria delle Carceri. When the Crusader who brought the Virgin's girdle back to Prato hid it under his mattress, angels levitated his bed, retrieved the relic and flew it to the bishop. San Galgano even has a sword in the stone, plunged there by a soldier after St Michael appeared to him, ordering him to renounce his warrior ways and become a holy hermit.

TOP 10
RELICS IN TUSCANY

1 Virgin's Girdle (Prato, Duomo, *see p59*)

2 Volto Santo (Lucca, Duomo)

3 Thorn from Christ's Crown (Pisa, Santa Maria della Spina)

4 Madonna del Voto (Siena, Duomo)

5 Head of St Catherine (Siena, San Domenico)

6 Crucifix (Florence, Santa Trinita)

7 Piece of the True Cross (Impruneta, Collegiata)

8 Sword in the Stone (San Galgano, *see p116*)

9 Rib of a Dragon (Tirli)

10 Galileo's Finger (Florence, Science Museum)

The journey by boat of the girdle said to have been worn by the Virgin is depicted here. The country that gave the world Roman Catholicism is rich in many such artifacts that are imbued with miraculous qualities.

TOP 10 ★ Siena's Campo and Palazzo Pubblico

The Piazza del Campo, affectionately called Il Campo, is one of Europe's loveliest squares, where crowds turn out to stroll and gossip. It has been the centre of Sienese public life since it was laid out atop the city's Roman Forum in 1100. The governmental Palazzo Pubblico, with its graceful tower, was added in 1297, and the curve of brick buildings opposite built to match. The Palazzo houses the Museo Civico. Twice a year, the Campo is packed with crowds for the Palio.

set the style for the rest of the square.

3 Museo Civico: Fresco Cycle

Ambrogio Lorenzetti's *Allegory of Good and Bad Government* **(left)**, the greatest secular medieval fresco cycle in Europe, decorates the old city council chamber.

1 Palazzo Pubblico

The civic palace (1297–1310), with its graceful brickwork, three-light windows and medieval crenellations, set the standard for Sienese architecture **(centre)**. Its rooms now host the Museo Civico (see p36).

2 Palazzo Sansedoni

The oldest building on the Campo, its curving 13th-century façade **(below)**

4 Museo Civico: Guidoriccio da Fogliano

This 1330 fresco (see p36) is Simone Martini's greatest – though some challenge its authorship. The austere Maremma landscape, where nobleman Guidoriccio da Fogliano has just quashed the Montemassi rebellion, is charming.

5 Piazza del Campo

The square's nine sections honour the medieval ruling Council of Nine. Its fountain and slope are more than decorative: they're integral to the city's water system.

SIENA'S CONTRADE

The Campo is common ground for Siena's 17 traditional *contrade*, or wards. The Sienese are citizens of their *contrada* first, Siena second and Italy third. They are baptized in the *contrada* church, and should marry within their *contrada*; the *contrada* helps them in business, acts as their social club and mourns their deaths like family. The *contrade* do not tolerate crime, giving the town one of Europe's lowest crime rates. *Contrade* rivalries are played out here in the annual Palio horse race (see p76).

6 Loggia della Mercanzia

A commercial tribunal once held court under this 1417 loggia, which is decorated with sculptures by Vecchietta and Federighi. The tribunal judges were so famously impartial that governments from across Europe brought their financial disputes to be heard here.

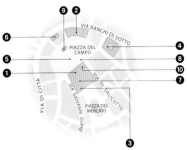

Plan of the Campo

10 Torre del Mangia

At 102 m (336 ft), this is one of the tallest medieval towers in Italy (left). There are 503 steps to the top – worth the effort for the stunning view.

NEED TO KNOW

MAP E4 ■ Tourist office: Piazza del Campo 56 ■ 0577 280 551 ■ www.terresiena.it

Palazzo Pubblico: open 10am–7pm daily (until 6pm in winter). Adm: €9

Torre del Mangia: open 10am–7pm daily (until 4pm Oct–mid-Mar). Adm: €10

Palazzo Piccolomini: open 9am–1pm Mon–Sat (by guided tour only)

■ Try one of the pricey cafés that ring the Campo, sometimes worth it for the pleasure of sipping a cappuccino at an outdoor table. Or head to Nannini, Siena's top café, just north of the Campo (see p98).

■ Behind the Palazzo Pubblico, Gino Cacino di Angelo (Piazza Mercato 31) is a great deli for buying sandwiches and other delicious snacks such as salami trays.

7 Palazzo Piccolomini

Housed in Siena's only Florentine Renaissance palace are the "Tavolette di Biccherna", municipal ledgers from the 13th century, with covers by Sano di Pietro, Ambrogio Lorenzetti, Domenico Beccafumi and others.

8 Cappella della Piazza

When the Black Death of 1348 finally abated, the third of Sienese citizens who survived built this marble loggia, with detailed, pretty stone carvings, to give thanks for their deliverance – and to pray against a repeat of the plague.

9 Fonte Gaia

The felicitous "Fountain of Joy" (left) is pretty, but it is merely a mediocre 19th-century reproduction of the original, whose weathered carvings by Jacopo della Quercia are now housed in the Santa Maria della Scala (see p32).

Siena's Museo Civico

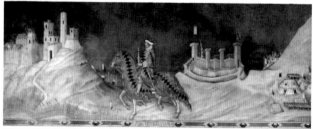

Simone Martini's fresco *Guidoriccio da Fogliano*, Sala del Mappamondo

1 Sala del Mappamondo
Across from Simone Martini's *Guidoriccio da Fogliano* (see p34) is his impressive *Maestà* (1315). Among the frescoes is a monochrome 15th-century battle scene.

2 Sala della Pace
Contains medieval Europe's greatest secular fresco by Lorenzetti, full of everyday life details (see p34).

Lorenzetti fresco, Sala della Pace

3 Cappella
This evocative room was frescoed by the Siennese pre-Renaissance artist Taddeo di Bartolo. Beyond an ornate screen is a fine altarpiece by Sodoma.

4 Anticappella
Taddeo di Bartolo also worked on the antechapel from 1415. His theme was civic virtue.

5 Sala di Balia
Spinello Aretino and his son teamed up (1407–8) to illustrate the life of Pope Alexander III, featuring a fantastic naval battle.

6 Sala del Risorgimento
The room boasts 19th-century sculptures and murals on the life of King Vittorio Emanuele II, who unified Italy.

7 Sala del Concistoro
Delegates attended government meetings beneath the ceiling frescoes by Beccafumi until 1786.

8 Anticamera del Concistoro
An Ambrogio Lorenzetti fresco is among the treasures here.

9 Vestibule
This is only a passageway, but it houses a 1429 gilded bronze she-wolf honouring Siena's Roman origins, as well as a fresco by Ambrogio Lorenzetti.

10 16th- to 18th-Century Paintings
The first rooms you come to contain a collection of paintings but don't spend too much time here.

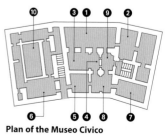

Plan of the Museo Civico

SIENESE ART

Birth of the Virgin by Pietro Lorenzetti

For a short time, Siena was as much a centre of artistic innovation as Florence, but sadly it was not destined to play such a big part in the Renaissance. Late 13th-century Sienese art came into its own as artists such as the painter Duccio started softening and enlivening the prevailing static Byzantine style with Gothic flowing lines and expressive features. By the early 14th century, Simone Martini and the Lorenzetti brothers were adding rich colour palettes and a penchant for intricate patterns to the mix. However, whereas Florence's Renaissance went on to revolutionize painting throughout Italy, the idiosyncratic Gothic style of Siena was dealt a crippling blow by the Black Death of 1348. The Lorenzettis died along with two-thirds of the population. A city concerned with rebuilding its economy and fending off Florentine expansion had no time or money for art. By the time Siena got back on its feet, local artists were following a variety of styles, from Gothic to Mannerist.

TOP 10 SIENESE ARTISTS

1 Simone Martini (1284–1344)

2 Duccio di Buoninsegna (1260–1319)

3 Ambrogio Lorenzetti (active 1319–48)

4 Pietro Lorenzetti (active 1306–48)

5 Domenico Beccafumi (1484–1551)

6 Sodoma (Giovanni Antonio Bazzi; 1477–1549)

7 Jacopo della Quercia (1371–1438)

8 Sassetta (1390–1450)

9 Francesco di Giorgio Martini (1439–1502)

10 Giovanni Duprè (1817–82)

Apparition on the Lake of Tiberiade is one of many scenes on the verso of Duccio's *Maestà* altarpiece, parts of which are now in Siena's cathedral museum.

TOP 10 ⭐ Chianti

The 50 km (30 miles) between Florence and Siena is a storybook landscape straight out of the background of a Renaissance painting: steeply rolling hills terraced with vineyards and olive groves, crenellated castles and bustling market towns. The seductive beauty of this Tuscan Arcadia has drawn people since Etruscan times; indeed, today it is so popular with the English that it has earned the nickname Chiantishire.

Castello di Brolio

A vineyard since 1007, Brolio **(right)** has been the soul of the Chianti region since the "Iron Baron" Bettino Ricasoli *(see p70)* perfected the Chianti wine formula in the 19th century.

② Greve in Chianti

This town has become Chianti's unofficial capital. There are wine shops galore, but the most popular spot is Falorni **(below)**, one of Italy's great butchers, stuffed with hanging prosciutto, aged cheeses and free samples.

③ Radda in Chianti

The only hilltop member of the Chianti League is capped by the 15th-century Palazzo del Podestà, studded with coats of arms of past mayors and offering good views. There's a good butcher/grocer's here as well: Luciano Prociatti.

④ Montefioralle

This 14th-century hamlet, hovering above Greve, consists of a single circular street, two churches and fantastic views over the valley and on to the 10th-century Pieve di San Cresci church below the walls.

⑤ Ipogeo di Montecalvario

This is a perfect 6th-century-BC tomb, with four passages tunnelling into the burial chambers. Visitors pay no entrance fee.

Pieve di San Leolino ⑥

Just south of Panzano is this little Romanesque church with Sienese paintings **(right)** from the 13th–15th centuries and a pretty brick cloister.

⑦ Panzano in Chianti

This often-overlooked town is the home of Dario Cecchini, arguably Italy's best butcher, and a couple of fine *enoteche*, where visitors can sample the local wines paired with snacks.

8 Castellina in Chianti

The most medieval of the Chianti League towns, this boasts a glowering Rocca fortress. Via della Volte, a tunnel-like road pierced by "windows" overlooking the countryside, was a soldiers' walk when this was Florence's last outpost before Siena.

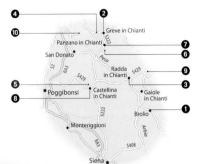

GETTING AROUND

The classic Chianti route is the S222 from Florence to Castellina; either zip straight down to Siena or explore more (highly recommended) by heading east on the S429 through Radda and Gaiole before you turn south on the S408 for Siena. But that only takes in the highlights. To truly get a feel for Chianti, take the back roads to Passignano, Coltibuono and other towns off the beaten path. Infrequent bus services also connect the main towns.

9 Badia a Coltibuono

This abbey from 770 includes an 11th-century church, Lorenza de' Medici's cookery school *(see p137)* and a classy restaurant run by her son Paolo.

NEED TO KNOW

MAP E3 ■ Tourist office: Piazza Giacomo Matteotti 10, Greve in Chianti ■ 055 854 6299

■ A good number of local vineyards *(see pp40–41)* host wine tastings with small snacks.

■ You can put together a picnic fit for the gods at butchers such as Falorni in Greve *(see p92)* and Prociatti in Radda.

■ Email or call in advance if you plan to visit a vineyard; find out the hours they accept visitors, whether they offer tours (and whether they're free), and ask if you need to book a tour or make a tasting appointment.

10 Badia a Passignano

The Antinori wine empire owns the vineyards around this 11th-century monastery **(below)**, which holds Baroque paintings by Ridolfo Ghirlandaio and local boy Il Passignano in the San Michele chapel, as well as Domenico and Davide Ghirlandaio's *Last Supper* fresco.

Chianti Vineyards

Castello di Brolio winery

1 Castello di Brolio
MAP E4 ■ 0577 7301

■ www.ricasoli.it

The estate that invented modern Chianti Classico is back in the Ricasoli family's hands. Book tours in advance (see p70).

2 Monsanto
MAP E3 ■ 055 805 9000

■ www.castellodimonsanto.it

This estate makes a 100 per cent Sangiovese Chianti. Call to tour the cellars (see p70).

3 Fonterutoli
MAP E3 ■ 0577 741 385

■ www.mazzei.it

Highly regarded estate in the Marquis Mazzei family since 1435. Excellent Chianti Classico, Badiola Sangioveto and Belguardo (a Morellino). Tastings available (see p71).

4 Castello di Ama
MAP E3 ■ 0577 746 031

■ www.castellodiama.com

Visitors can tour the estate, then taste and buy Castello di Ama's wines at Rinaldi Palmira's *enoteca* in nearby Lecchi.

5 Castello di Volpaia
MAP E3 ■ 0577 738 066

■ www.volpaia.it

Visit the 13th-century village around an imposing central tower, and taste wines, oils and vinegars. Book tours a week ahead.

6 Castello Vicchiomaggio
MAP E3 ■ 055 854 079

■ www.vicchiomaggio.it

This enterprising estate offers tastings, cellar tours (notice required) and cooking lessons on request. There is also a trattoria in the castle.

7 Villa Vignamaggio
MAP E3 ■ 055 854 661

■ www.vignamaggio.com

A historic villa (see p64 & p147) whose wines were the first to be called Chianti. Book ahead for tours.

8 Villa Vistarenni
MAP E3 ■ 0577 738 186

■ www.villavistarenni.com

Modern cellars, a 17th-century villa and scenic vineyards, with tastings for small groups who book a day in advance.

9 Rocca delle Macie
MAP E3 ■ 0577 732 236

■ www.roccadellemacie.com

A summer opera festival enlivens this estate, which also offers accommodation in 14th-century farm buildings.

10 Castello di Verrazzano
MAP E3 ■ 055 854 243

■ www.verrazzano.com

Rocca delle Macie

The family has been making wine since 1100. Sample it at the estate from Monday to Saturday.

Wine barrels, Castello di Verrazzano

THE STORY OF CHIANTI CLASSICO

Black Cockerel seal

Wine from the Chianti hills has been enjoyed at least since Roman times (one of its grapes, the Canaiolo, was cultivated by the Etruscans). It's been called Chianti since 1404, when a barrel was sent beyond the area to Prato. A political "Chianti League" of towns was formed in the 13th century, but it took a 1716 grand ducal decree to establish this as the world's first officially defined wine-producing region. In 1960, Chianti became the first Italian "DOCG" – the highest mark of quality. Some 70 sq km (27 sq miles) are strung with the grapes – two reds (Sangiovese and Canaiolo) and two whites (Malvasia and Trebbiano) – that make Chianti Classico. Though there are seven Chianti-producing regions, only wines produced in the Chianti hills may be called Classico and carry the seal of the Black Cockerel.

TOP 10 RECENT VINTAGES

1 2013
2 2010
3 2009
4 2008
5 2007
6 2006
7 2004
8 2001
9 1999
10 1997

Chianti Vineyards

Many vineyards allow you to sample their wares, and a bottle bought direct from the maker is a wonderful souvenir – or a treat for a picnic.

The villa and vineyards of the Villa Vistarenni estate

TOP 10 ⭐ Cortona

One of Tuscany's most rewarding hill towns, Cortona is a trove of Etruscan tombs, medieval alleyways, Renaissance art, sweeping views and small-town ambience. It was probably settled even before the Etruscans, and later became an important member of that society, as the tombs in its valley attest. The birthplace of Fra Angelico, Cortona also produced the Renaissance genius Luca Signorelli, the Baroque master Pietro da Cortona and the 20th-century Futurist Gino Severini.

3 Museo Diocesano

This small museum has outstanding works, from a Roman sarcophagus, studied by Donatello, to art by Pietro Lorenzetti, Fra Angelico, Francesco Signorelli and his uncle Luca, whose *Communion of the Apostles* **(right)** is held by the museum.

1 Museo dell' Accademia Etrusca

This museum **(above)** was revamped in 2008 to expand the exhibits on Roman and Etruscan Cortona, including finds from the excavations at Melone del Sodo (I and II) plus a multimedia section. The star attraction in the original halls upstairs is a 5th-century-BC Medusa bronze lamp. The eclectic collection also includes paintings by Luca Signorelli and Pinturicchio, Egyptian finds and a section on Futurist Gino Severini.

4 San Niccolò

A tiny 15th-century church beyond a cypress-lined courtyard, housing a two-sided altarpiece by Luca Signorelli (ring the bell and ask the custodian to flip it for you).

5 Rugapiana (Via Nazionale)

The main drag of Cortona is the only flat street (*rugapiana* in local dialect) in town. Steep alleyways spill off from either side of this narrow, flagstoned, pedestrianized thoroughfare.

6 Melone I del Sodo

The passages of this 6th-century-BC Etruscan tomb were shored up in the 1800s. Visitors are also able to view the remarkable adjoining burial chambers and Etruscan script.

2 Duomo

Cortona's barrel-vaulted Renaissance cathedral **(right)** is filled with paintings from the 16th and 17th centuries by Luca Signorelli and other artists.

⑦ Santa Maria delle Grazie al Calcinaio

An architectural set piece of the High Renaissance, Santa Maria (1485–1513) is the masterpiece of Francesco di Giorgio Martini, set amid olive groves below the town walls **(left)**.

CORTONA ORIENTATION

The road up to the hill town starts near the Melone tombs down on the valley floor. It winds up through olive groves, passing the Tomba di Pitagora and Santa Maria church, before terminating at the bus stop square of Piazza Garibaldi. From here, Via Nazionale leads into the heart of town – the piazzas Repubblica and Signorelli – close to most other sights.

⑧ Melone II del Sodo

The remarkable altar on this huge 6th-century-BC Etruscan tumulus was discovered in the 1990s. The altar – a sphinx-flanked staircase leading to a wide platform – is orientated towards Cortona up on the hillside, suggesting that this may have been the resting place of a prince.

⑨ San Domenico

The church boasts a faded Fra Angelico lunette fresco of the Madonna over the entrance, a Luca Signorelli *Madonna* inside, and a huge, glittering 15th-century Lorenzo di Niccolò altarpiece that is entirely intact (a rarity).

⑩ Tomba di Pitagora

The dirt hillock covering this 3rd-century-BC tomb **(below)** was removed long ago. The stone chamber was erroneously dubbed "Pythagoras' Tomb" when somebody confused Cortona with the mathematician's hometown, Crotone, in Calabria.

NEED TO KNOW

MAP F4 ▪ Tourist office: Piazza Signorelli 9 ▪ 0575 637 223 ▪ www.cortonaweb.net

Museo dell'Accademia Etrusca: Nov–Mar: closed Mon. Adm: €10

Museo Diocesano: closed Mon (Nov–Mar). Adm: €5

Melone II del Sodo: 8:30am–1:30pm Tue–Sun.

▪ Enoteca Enotria (Via Nazionale 81) offers laid-back wine tastings that are accompanied by cheese, local *ciaccia* (bread) and *salumi* (cured meats).

▪ Follow Via Santa Margherita as it winds steeply up past gardens and Severini-designed shrines to the 16th-century hilltop Fortezza Medicea di Girifalco for sweeping views over the Val di Chiana to Lake Trasimeno.

Etruscan Sights Around Cortona and Beyond

1 Cortona: Museo dell'Accademia Etrusca

Cortona's best museum has a number of superb Etruscan and Cortonese artifacts (see p42).

2 Cortona: Tombs

Etruscan tombs in the valley below Cortona include the two "Melone" tombs, and the Tomba di Pitagora (see pp42–3).

3 Volterra: Museo Etrusco Guarnacci

Etruscans transformed this 9th-century-BC town into part of the Dodecapolis confederation. Over 600 marvellous funerary urns fill the museum (see p55), which also preserves the Shade of the Evening, an elegantly elongated bronze sculpture of a boy.

4 Sovana: Tombs and Vie Cave

Six necropolises surround this Etruscan settlement (see p128 & p130), most of them romantically overgrown. The vie cave are narrow paths carved up to 20 m (65 ft) deep – their function is unknown.

5 Florence: Museo Archeologico

Along with riches from Ancient Rome and Antioch, Florence's oft-overlooked archaeology museum preserves one of the greatest artworks from Etruria, a large, 4th-century-BC bronze chimera, probably cast in Chiusi or Orvieto (see p84).

6 Populonia

Ancient coastal smelting centre (see p128). The medieval town has a small museum and some ancient walls. A nearby necropolis illustrates changing

Etruscan tomb in Populonia

tomb styles, from simple passages to domed tumuli (barrows) to edicola (shrine-type tombs).

7 Chiusi: Museo Archeologico Nazionale Etrusco

This excellent museum houses fine jars and funerary urns, some with miraculously preserved polychrome painting (see p122).

8 Chiusi: Tombs

A custodian from Chiusi museum will accompany you to unlock two of the tombs dotting Chiusi's valley, including the Tomba della Pellegrina with its urns and sarcophagi still in place (see p122).

9 Grosseto: Museo Civico Archeologico

Many artifacts found in the Maremma (Sovana, Roselle, Vetulonia), such as terracotta reliefs and painted vases (see p128), have made their way here.

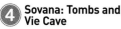

Cooking pot, Grosseto

10 Roselle

 The only fully excavated Etruscan town in Tuscany. It was once part of Dodecapolis but was conquered early (294 BC). The remains of Etruscan walls and houses lie next to a Roman amphi-theatre and baths.

THE ETRUSCANS

Tuscany is named after the Etruscans who settled central Italy, from Northern Lazio to the Umbrian Apennines, around the 8th century BC. Little is known about them beyond scant Roman records (the early Roman Tarquin kings were actually Etruscan) and the artifacts that have survived, of which most are funerary. According to myth, they came from Asia Minor (bringing with them Tuscany's familiar cypress tree), enjoyed an advanced culture, with relative equality between the sexes, and excelled at engineering – Etruscans taught the Romans the art of draining land for agriculture. They traded extensively with the Greeks, who had settled southern Italy; much Etruscan-era painted pottery is either Greek- or Attic-influenced, and the analphabetic Etruscans quickly adopted Greek letters. Their 12 greatest city-states formed a loose and somewhat fluctuating confederation called Dodecapolis. By the 3rd century BC, expansion-hungry Romans began conquering Etruria, replacing Etruscan hill towns with Roman valley camps and ruler-straight roads.

TOP 10
TOWNS FOUNDED BY THE ETRUSCANS

1 Volterra (Map D4)
2 Arezzo (Map F3)
3 Chiusi (Map F5)
4 Cortona (Map F4)
5 Fiesole (Map E2)
6 Pitigliano (Map F6)
7 Sovana (Map F6)
8 Populonia (Map C5)
9 Saturnia (Map E6)
10 Roselle (Map E5)

Etruscan alabaster funerary urn in Volterra's Museo Etrusco Guarnacci

The remains of an Etruscan settlement at Roselle

TOP 10 ⭐ Lucca

Lucca is an elegant city of opera and olive oil, Romanesque churches and hidden palace gardens. Its historic centre is contained within massive 16th-century redbrick bastions. The street plan first laid down by the Romans is little altered – in the Middle Ages the ancient amphitheatre was used as a foundation for houses. The composers Boccherini and Puccini were born here, and are celebrated in concerts around the city. More contemporary acts play at the town's renowned annual summer music festival.

Duomo ②
The early 13th-century façade **(right)** stacks Pisan-Romanesque arcades above a portico with Romanesque carvings. Inside are sculptures by 15th-century master Matteo Civitale, Jacopo della Quercia's Tomb of Ilaria, Tintoretto's *Last Supper* (1591) and the revered *Volto Santo di Lucca*, supposedly carved by Nicodemus.

① San Michele in Foro
Built atop the Roman Forum, San Michele's Pisan-Romanesque arcades **(above)** are stacked even higher than the Duomo's. Inside are a *Madonna and Child* by Civitale, another by Andrea della Robbia, and a Filippino Lippi *Saints*. Composer Puccini was a chorister here.

③ Tomb of Ilaria
Jacopo della Quercia's masterpiece (1405–7) in the sacristy of the Duomo marries the medieval lying-in-state pose of town boss Paolo Guinigi's young wife (she died at 26) with classical-inspired garlands and cherubs. Jacopo's delicate chisel turned hard marble into soft cushions and captured Ilaria's ethereal beauty.

④ Piazza Anfiteatro
Lucca's Roman amphitheatre was long ago mined for building stone, but its oval remained as a base for medieval houses. It is now a quiet piazza, with ancient arches still embedded in house walls **(below)**.

7 Basilica di San Frediano

Treasures here include a Romanesque font and Amico Aspertini's 1508–9 frescoes, the *Miracles of San Frediano*. The façade glitters with Byzantine mosaics **(above)**.

8 The Walls

Chestnuts and umbrella pines shade the gravelly path atop the remarkable ramparts (1544–1650). Locals love to stroll or bicycle here for views into gardens or out over the Apuan Alps.

9 Museo Nazionale di Palazzo Mansi

Riotous Baroque palace interiors serve as the backdrop for Mannerist and Renaissance art by Bronzino, Beccafumi, Correggio, Sodoma and Luca Giordano.

5 Museo Nazionale Villa Guinigi

This 15th-century villa houses a fine archaeology section containing Iron Age, Ligurian and later Etruscan finds, decent Renaissance paintings and wood inlay from the 15th century.

6 Santa Maria Forisportam

Though the Pisan façade is 12th-century, the interior is mostly 17th-century, including two Guercino altarpieces and a *pietre dure* ciborium (inlaid stone vessel).

10 Torre Guinigi

The 14th-century palace of Lucca's ruling family sprouts a 44-m (144-ft) tower offering stunning views **(below)**.

LUCCA'S HISTORY

Villa Guinigi's collections show the region's Stone Age history, but the town was founded by the Romans. Caesar, Pompey and Crassus cemented their First Triumvirate here. St Peter's disciple Paulinus legendarily brought Christianity to Lucca, and it was a waypoint on the Via Francigena pilgrim route. The tough Marquess Mathilda ruled the town during the Lombard period. Succeeded by local lords – except during one 14th-century stint under Pisa – Lucca remained proudly independent of Florence until Napoleon gave the city to his sister Elisa in 1805.

NEED TO KNOW

MAP C2 ▪ Tourist office: Piazzale Verdi ▪ 0583 583 150 ▪ www.luccaturismo.it

Duomo: open daily. Adm for Tomb of Ilaria

San Frediano: open daily

Torre Guinigi: open daily. Adm

Museo Nazionale di Palazzo Mansi: closed Mon. Adm

Museo Nazionale Villa Guinigi: closed Mon. Adm; combined ticket also allows access to both museums

▪ Da Leo *(see p113)* serves delicious cakes, as well as some more substantial local dishes.

▪ The Lucchesi are avid cyclists; there are several rental places on Piazza Santa Maria.

The Top 10 of Everything

Medieval towers rise above
the town of San Gimignano

📊 Medici Rulers

Giovanni di Bicci by dell'Altissimo

1 Giovanni di Bicci (1360–1429)

Founded the Medici fortune by making his family's bank the bank for the papal Curia. He also served as head of the *Priori* government of Florence and was a sponsor of Ghiberti's Baptistry commission.

2 Cosimo il Vecchio (1389–1464)

Cosimo the Elder adroitly managed his family fortune, political clout and personal image to become the *de facto* ruler of Florence. Each time he was exiled or imprisoned by rivals, popular sentiment brought him back to power.

3 Lorenzo the Magnificent (1449–92)

Most beloved of the Medici. A devout humanist and patron of the arts (as well as a fair poet himself) who, alongside many accomplishments of his own, sponsored Michelangelo's early career. A skilled diplomat and able ruler of the city.

4 Pope Leo X (Giovanni; 1475–1521)

Lorenzo the Magnificent's son called the shots from Rome, exclaiming "God has risen us to the papacy; let us enjoy it." The younger brother and nephews he groomed to take over Florence all died, and so his cousin, Cardinal Giulio, took the reins.

5 Pope Clement VII (Giulio; 1478–1534)

Cardinal Giulio fared well when running Florence himself, but upon becoming pope spent his energies fighting Emperor Charles V, leaving Florence to the incompetent young Medicis Alessandro and Ippolito.

6 Alessandro (1510–37)

Clement VII's illegitimate son inherited the ducal mantle at the age of 19, and soon became a despot, carousing with his cousin Lorenzino, who eventually grew jealous and murdered Alessandro.

Statue of Cosimo I by Giambologna

7 Cosimo I (1519–74)

The first Medici to gain the title of grand duke, Cosimo became a duke at the age of 17, when the first primary Medici line petered out. He conquered Siena, built a port (Livorno) and ruled judiciously but with something of an iron fist.

8 Ferdinando I (1549–1609)

Popular, hands-on grand duke who founded hospitals, gave dowries to girls from poor families, promoted agriculture and hosted grand parties. He married Christine of Lorraine, whose family would eventually inherit the grand ducal title.

9 Anna Maria (1667–1743)

The last of the main Medici line, along with her brother Gian Gastone. She willed all Medici possessions – including the Uffizi, Pitti and Bargello collections – to the Lorraine grand dukes on the stipulation the patrimony could never be removed from Florence.

Portrait of Anna Maria by Jacob Voet

10 Gian Gastone (1671–1737)

The last Medici ruler reversed many of his predecessor's policies. He revoked the ban on the teaching of the "new ideas" of philosophers such as Galileo and repealed laws that placed restrictions on Jews. In his later years, he became an obese sensualist who rarely stirred from bed, where he frequently cavorted with nubile young men. With his demise the grand ducal title passed to the Austrian Lorraines.

Bust of Gian Gastone

TOP 10 WAYS THE MEDICI SUPPORTED THE ARTS

Lorenzo the Magnificent

1 Michelangelo
Lorenzo the Magnificent recruited the young artist to study the sculptures in the Medici gardens.

2 Donatello
Cosimo il Vecchio's will saw that the sculptor never lacked for commissions. Donatello is buried near Cosimo in the Basilica of San Lorenzo.

3 Galileo
Cosimo II protected the iconoclastic scientist from the Inquisition, and bargained his death sentence down to excommunication and house arrest.

4 Uffizi
Francesco I opened this gallery of the family's art collections on the third floor of their offices (see pp12–15).

5 Botticelli
A Medici cousin, probably influenced by Lorenzo de' Medici, commissioned the *Birth of Venus* and *La Primavera*.

6 Pitti Palace
The grand ducal home has works from the Medici collections (see pp18–21).

7 San Marco
Cosimo il Vecchio built the monastery, which included Europe's first public library (see p82).

8 World's First Opera
Ferdinando I commissioned *Dafne*, a story set to music, from Jacopo Peri and Ottavio Rinuccini for his wedding (1589).

9 Benvenuto Cellini
Cosimo I convinced Cellini to return to Florence to make his masterpiece, *Perseus with the Head of Medusa*.

10 Opificio delle Pietre Dure
Ferdinando I founded this inlaid stone workshop, also Florence's chief laboratory for art restoration.

Tuscan Masterpieces

1 David
Florence, Galleria dell'Accademia *(see p81)*

At the age of 26, Michelangelo took on a huge slab of marble, nicknamed "the Giant" by the sculptors of the day, and turned it into *David* (1501–4), an intense young man contemplating his task as a proper Renaissance humanist would. Intended for Florence's Duomo, it first stood in front of the Palazzo Vecchio. Damaged during an anti-Medici riot, it was eventually wheeled to the Accademia for safekeeping.

2 Birth of Venus
Florence, Uffizi *(see p12)*

Botticelli's beauty strikes a classical, modest pose, covering her nakedness with her hands while an *Ora* (handmaiden) rushes to clothe her and the west wind, Zephyr, blows her gracefully to shore in a swirl of pink roses (c.1484–6).

3 Rosso Fiorentino's Deposition
Volterra, Pinacoteca *(see p115)*

The garish colours and twisted poses are the classic hallmarks of

Michelangelo's *David*

Florentine Mannerism, and this is one of its masterpieces. This shockingly modern take on a traditional subject feels much more recent than 1521.

4 Gates of Paradise
Florence, Baptistry *(see p16)*

It took Ghiberti many years (1425–52) to complete ten gilded bronze panels of Old Testament scenes on the Baptistry's east doors (now copies; originals in the Museo dell'Opera).

5 Trinità
Florence, Santa Maria Novella *(see p56)*

Masaccio's *Trinità*, painted in 1428, is the first painting to use the mathematical single point perspective. The triangular composition of the work draws lines from the two kneeling donors straight through the halos of Mary and St John to God the Father.

6 Duccio's Maestà
Siena, Museo dell'Opera Metropolitana *(see p32)*

The first undisputed masterpiece of the Sienese School was Duccio's 1311 *Maestà*, an altarpiece composed of several individual paintings.

Duccio di Buoninsegna's *Maestà* depicting an enthroned Madonna and Child

It was paraded through the streets before its installation, and painting a *Maestà* became a rite of passage for Sienese artists.

7 Giovanni Pisano's Pulpit
Pistoia, Sant'Andrea *(see p89)*
The Pisanos (father and son) carved four great stone pulpits, in Pisa, Siena and Pistoia. Giovanni's hexagonal 1301 pulpit illustrates, in gory Gothic detail, biblical tales such as the "Massacre of the Innocents".

8 Giotto's Maestà
Florence, Uffizi *(see p12)*
Giotto's masterful work (1310) broke conventions by dressing the Virgin in normal clothes rather than stylized robes, with the Child perched on an actual lap rather than hovering.

9 Allegory of Good and Bad Government
Siena, Museo Civico *(see p34 & p36)*
Ambrogio Lorenzetti's 1338 fresco wraps around the medieval ruling Council of Nine's inner chamber. Ruled by the allegorical figures of Good Government, medieval Siena prospers, while ruled by Bad Government, it crumbles.

Lorenzetti's allegory of government

10 Resurrection of Christ
Sansepolcro, Museo Civico *(see p103)*
As Piero della Francesca's muscled, heavy-lidded Jesus rises from his sarcophagus, the dreary, dead landscape flowers into life (1463). The sleeping Roman soldier slumped in brown armour is said to be a self-portrait.

TOP 10 TUSCAN ARTISTS

Michelangelo **by del Conte**

1 Giotto *(1266–1337)*
Giotto took painting from its static, Byzantine style and set it on the road to the Renaissance.

2 Simone Martini *(1284–1344)*
Martini took a medieval eye for iconography and married it to a vibrant palette and intense drama.

3 Donatello *(1386–1466)*
The first Renaissance sculptor worked out perspective before the painters, and cast the first equestrian statue and first freestanding nude since antiquity.

4 Fra Angelico *(1395–1455)*
Manuscript illumination informed his art, but Angelico's work is based on the ideas of naturalism and perspective.

5 Masaccio *(1401–28)*
Masaccio imbued Renaissance painting with an unflinching naturalism and perfected single point perspective.

6 Piero della Francesca *(1416–92)*
A visionary whose compositions have an ethereal spirituality, well-modelled figures and a mastery of perspective.

7 Botticelli *(1444–1510)*
The master of grand mythological scenes is said to have tossed his own "blasphemous" works upon the Bonfire of the Vanities *(see p82)*.

8 Leonardo da Vinci *(1452–1519)*
The ultimate Renaissance Man: a painter, proto-scientist and inventor, with a penchant for experimentation.

9 Michelangelo *(1475–1564)*
Famously irascible, he was a sculptor of genius by his early 20s.

10 Pontormo *(1494–1557)*
Pontormo took the use of non-primary colours and experimentation with figures to vivid and complex extremes.

Museums

1 Florence's Uffizi

Botticelli's *Birth of Venus*, Leonardo's *Annunciation* and Michelangelo's *Tondo Doni* are just three of the masterpieces that make this the top sight in all of Tuscany (see pp12–15).

2 Florence's Pitti Palace

The Galleria Palatina features Raphael Madonnas and Titian beauties alongside works by Andrea del Sarto, Perugino, Signorelli, Caravaggio and Rubens. Palatial décor is the backdrop to collections of costumes, silverware and carriages (see pp18–21).

3 Siena's Museo Civico

A battlemented medieval town hall with the best Gothic painting in Siena (see p36), including Lorenzetti's incomparable *Allegory of Good and Bad Government*.

4 Florence's Bargello

Italy's top sculpture gallery (see p82) is set in a former town hall and prison dating to 1255, and takes its name from the office of the city's police chief or *bargello* that was once based here. The gallery contains the world's best collection of Donatellos. It also holds sculptures by Cellini, Giambologna and Michelangelo.

5 Cortona's Museo dell'Accademia Etrusca

MAP F4 ■ Piazza Signorelli ■ Open 10am–7pm Tue–Sun (to 5pm Nov–Mar) ■ Adm

This wonderful collection preserves Etruscan finds as well as Renaissance and Baroque paintings, a few Egyptian artifacts, decorative arts and works by the prominent Futurist artist Gino Severini who lived locally (see p44).

A gallery at the Accademia, Florence

6 Florence's Galleria dell'Accademia

MAP N1 ■ Via Ricasoli 60 ■ Open 8:15am–6:50pm Tue–Sun ■ Adm ■ www.galleriaaccademia firenze.beniculturali.it

The crowds come for Michelangelo's *David*, then stay for his *Slaves*, carved for the tomb of Julius II, and art by Botticelli, Lorenzo di Credi, Orcagna, Perugino and del Sarto (see p81).

7 Sansepolcro's Museo Civico

MAP F3 ■ Via Aggiunti 65 ■ Open 10am–1:30pm & 2:30–7pm daily Jun–Sep; 10am–1pm & 2:30–6pm Oct–May ■ Adm

Piero della Francesca's hometown (see p103) has retained some of his greatest, most psychologically penetrating works, including *Madonna della Misericordia* (1445–62), *San Giuliano* (1458) and the eerie *Resurrection* (1463), called "the best picture in the world" by Aldous Huxley in a 1925 essay.

Bronze Etruscan chandelier in Cortona's museum

8 Florence's Museo Galileo

MAP N5 ▪ Piazza dei Giudici 1 ▪ Open 9:30am–6pm Wed–Mon, 9:30am–1pm Tue ▪ Adm

The instruments displayed here are often as beautiful as they are scientifically significant. Exhibits include a mechanical "calculator" made of engraved disks, a perpetual motion machine and the telescopes with which Galileo discovered the moons of Jupiter.

9 Siena's Pinacoteca Nazionale

MAP E4 ▪ Via S Pietro 29 ▪ Open 8:15am–7:15pm Tue–Sat, 9am–1pm Sun & Mon ▪ Adm

Set in a 14th-century palazzo *(see p95)*, this is Tuscany's best survey of Sienese painting, and houses Bartolo di Fredi's *Adoration of the Magi*.

Adoration of the Magi by di Fredi

10 Volterra's Museo Etrusco Guarnacci

MAP D4 ▪ Via Don Minzoni 15 ▪ Open 9am–7pm daily (Nov–Mar: 10am–4:30pm) ▪ Adm

One of Tuscany's top Etruscan museums, with over 600 marble and alabaster funerary urns carved with myths or metaphors for the afterlife, a terracotta sarcophagus lid of an elderly couple, and small bronzes including the elongated boyish figure, *Shade of the Evening (see p44)*.

TOP 10 ARTISTIC STYLES

Macchiaioli-style work by Abbati

1 Etruscan
Heavily influenced by Greek art, the style is seen in large statues, funerary urns and bronze votives from the 8th to the 4th centuries BC.

2 Byzantine
Conservative, static, stylized in Eastern iconographic tradition of the 9th–13th centuries AD. Almond faces, large eyes, robes pleated in gold cross-hatching.

3 Gothic
More expressive, colourful and realistic than Byzantine. Flowing lines and dramatic gestures (13th–14th centuries).

4 Renaissance
Tuscany's greatest contribution to art history. In their elegant compositions, the 15th- and 16th-century Florentine artists developed a more naturalistic style as well as complex techniques such as perspective.

5 Mannerism
Late Renaissance, 16th-century offshoot based on Michelangelo's rich colour palette and twisting poses.

6 Baroque
Similar to Mannerism, but using strong contrasts of light and shade to achieve high drama (16th–17th centuries).

7 Rococo
Baroque gone chaotic, effusive and overwrought (18th century).

8 Neo-Classical
Based on classical models and mythological themes (19th century).

9 Macchiaioli
Tuscan cousin of Impressionism (late 19th century).

10 Liberty
Italian 20th-century Art Nouveau, seen mostly on façades and shop signs.

Churches in Florence

1 Duomo
See pp16–17.

2 Santa Maria Novella
MAP L2 ■ Piazza S Maria Novella ■ Open Apr–Sep: 9am–7pm daily (from 11am Fri); Oct–Mar: 9am–5:30pm Mon–Sat (from 11am Fri), 1–5pm Sun ■ Adm

Among the masterpieces here are Masaccio's 1428 *Trinità*, which had the first use of Renaissance perspective in a painting, Giotto's *Crucifix*, Filippino Lippi's *Cappella Strozzi* frescoes (1486) and Ghirlandaio's colourful sanctuary frescoes (1485). The greenish Noah frescoes (1446) are warped perspectives by Paolo Uccello.

3 Santa Croce
MAP P4–5 ■ Piazza S Croce ■ Open 9:30am–5pm Mon–Sat, 2–5pm Sun ■ Adm includes museum

Behind the striking marble façade is a Gothic pantheon of cultural heroes that contains the tombs of Machiavelli, Michelangelo, Rossini and Galileo (reburied here in 1737). Giotto frescoed the two chapels sited to the right of the altar *(see p82)*.

The interior of San Lorenzo

4 San Lorenzo and the Medici Chapels
MAP M2 ■ Piazza di S Lorenzo ■ Basilica: open 10am–5pm Mon–Sat, 1:30–5pm Sun (Mar–Oct); Medici Chapel: open 8:15am–5pm daily (closed 1st & 3rd Mon of month) ■ Adm

San Lorenzo was the Medici parish church. The tombs of the family are decorated by Donatello, Rosso Fiorentino, Bronzino and Filippo Lippi, with architecture by Brunelleschi (interior and Old Sacristy) and Michelangelo (Laurentian Library and New Sacristy). The New Sacristy contains Michelangelo's roughly finished *Dawn, Dusk, Day* and *Night*.

5 Santo Spirito
MAP L5 ■ Piazza S Spirito ■ Open 9:30am–12:30pm & 4–5:30pm Mon–Sat, 11:30am–12:30pm & 4–6:30pm Sun

Brunelleschi's Renaissance masterpiece has proportions picked out in clean lines of *pietra serena* stone against white plaster. Seek out altarpieces by Filippino Lippi (*Madonna and Child with Saints*, 1466) and Verrocchio (a minimalist *St Monica and Augustinian Nuns*).

Galileo's tomb in Santa Croce

The church of San Miniato al Monte

façade, while the artist Ghirlandaio frescoed the Cappella Sasetti with the *Life of St Francis* set in 15th-century Florence.

⑨ Orsanmichele

MAP M4 ■ Via dell'Arte della Lana ■ Open 10am–5pm Tue–Sun

This granary-turned-church, once used by the city's trade guilds, is ringed with statues by Donatello, Ghiberti and Verrocchio (all copies; the originals are in the museum upstairs). Orcagna designed the tabernacle to resemble a cathedral and it contains *Madonna and Child with Angels*, a 1348 work by Daddi.

⑥ San Miniato al Monte

MAP E3 ■ Via Monte alle Croci ■ Open 8am–1pm & 3:30–7pm Mon–Sat, 8am–7pm Sun (summer: 8am–7pm daily)

Perched high above the city, this is Florence's only Romanesque church. The doors of Michelozzo's tabernacle were painted by Agnolo Gaddi (1394–6), one of the last Florentine artists stylistically descended from Giotto.

⑦ Santa Maria del Carmine

MAP K4 ■ Piazza del Carmine ■ Open 10am–5pm Mon–Sat, 1–5pm Sun ■ Adm for Brancacci Chapel

Masolino started the Brancacci Chapel's frescoes of St Peter's life in 1424. Another of his works, *Adam and Eve*, is rather sweet compared to the powerful *Expulsion from the Garden* by his successor, Masaccio. Filippino Lippi completed the cycle in 1485.

⑧ Santa Trinita

MAP L4 ■ Piazza S Trinita ■ Open 8am–noon & 4–6pm Mon–Sat, 4–6pm Sun

Florentine artist and architect Buontalenti provided the Mannerist

Statue of St George, Orsanmichele

⑩ Santissima Annunziata

MAP P1 ■ Piazza SS Annunziata ■ Open 7:30am–12:30pm & 4–6:30pm daily

The Michelozzo-designed entry cloister was frescoed by Mannerists Andrea del Sarto, Rosso and Pontormo. The octagonal Baroque tribune is decorated with Perugino's *Madonna and Saints* and Bronzino's *Resurrection*. In the back chapel, sculptures by Giambologna himself adorn his tomb.

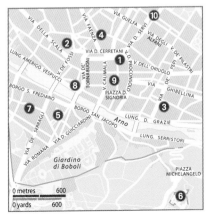

🔟 Churches outside Florence

Detail of the portal at Massa Marittima's Duomo

① Siena's Duomo

A striped Romanesque-Gothic pile, richly decorated by Giovanni Pisano, Pinturicchio, Donatello, Michelangelo, Beccafumi and Bernini *(see pp30–31)*.

② San Gimignano's Collegiata

MAP D3 ▪ Piazza del Duomo ▪ Apr–Oct: 10am–7:30pm Mon–Fri, 10am–5:30pm Sat, 12:30–7:30pm Sun; Nov–Mar: 10am–5pm Mon–Sat, 12:30–5pm Sun ▪ Closed during religious services; 1 & 31 Jan, 12 Mar, 1st Sun in Aug, 25 Dec ▪ Adm

The medieval Manhattan's main church is covered inside with 14th- and 15th-century frescoes, including a cycle by Ghirlandaio *(see p24)*.

③ Pisa's Duomo

Apart from the Pisan-Romanesque exterior, only a few elements, such as Cimabue's apse mosaic of 1302, survived a 1595 fire. However, the late Renaissance/early Baroque refurbishment was stylish, and local legend holds the swinging of the nave's large bronze lamp inspired Galileo's Law of Pendulums *(see pp26–9)*.

④ Lucca's Duomo

MAP C2 ▪ Piazza San Martino ▪ Open 9am–7pm daily

San Martino is a masterpiece of Romanesque stacked open arcades, stuffed with sculpture from Gothic reliefs to works by two great 15th-century talents, local Matteo Civitale and Sienese Jacopo della Quercia *(see p46)*.

⑤ Massa Marittima's Duomo

MAP D4/5 ▪ Piazza Garibaldi ▪ Open 8am–noon & 3–6pm

A cathedral with a split personality, this boasts Romanesque arcading topped by Gothic pinnacles and bell tower. It houses some wonderfully idiosyncratic sculpture: three takes on the life of local patron San Cerbone as well as lovely pre-Romanesque carvings.

⑥ Sant'Antimo

MAP E5 ▪ Abbazia di Sant'Antimo ▪ Open 10:15am–12:30pm & 3–6:30pm Mon–Sat, 9:15–10:45am & 3–6pm Sun

Although this isolated Cistercian abbey was founded by Charlemagne, the present building dates only from 1118. Inside are several beautifully carved column capitals. Monks pray in chant five times daily; ask them to see the sacristy's earthy frescoes *(see p121)*.

The abbey of Sant'Antimo

7 Arezzo's San Francesco

MAP F3 ▪ Piazza S Francesco ▪ Open 9am–7pm Mon–Fri, 9am–6pm Sat, 1–6pm Sun (to 5:30pm Sat & Sun in winter); advance booking needed (0575 352 727 or online) ▪ Adm for Piero frescoes ▪ www.pierodella francesca.it

A 15-year restoration of the choir's *Legend of the True Cross* (1448–66), the greatest fresco cycle by Piero della Francesca, has revived its vitality and vibrancy *(see p103)*.

8 Pienza's Duomo

MAP F4 ▪ Piazza Pio II ▪ Open 7am–1pm & 2:30–7pm

Behind the Classical façade is a reinterpreted German Gothic hall church building, the result of Piccolomini Pope Pius II's interference in Rossellino's initial plan to build the perfect Renaissance town *(see p121)*.

9 Pistoia's Duomo

MAP D2 ▪ Piazza del Duomo ▪ Open 8:30am–12:30pm & 3:30–7pm ▪ Adm for St Jacopo's chapel

Andrea della Robbia's enamelled terracotta entrance accents the zebra stripes of the

St Nicholas at Pienza's Duomo

Romanesque exterior. The Altar of St Jacopo (1287–1456) contains some of Italy's finest silversmithing. Ask the custodian to show you Verrocchio's striking 1485 *Madonna di Piazza (see p89)*.

10 Prato's Duomo

MAP D2 ▪ Piazza Duomo ▪ Open 7:30am–7pm Mon–Sat, 7:30am–noon & 1–7pm Sun

Michelozzo's outside pulpit ensures that crowds in the piazza are able to see the bishop display the Virgin's girdle *(see p33)*. Fra Filippo Lippi's graceful frescoes in the choir are considered his most important works and include the famous scene of Salomé holding the head of John the Baptist on a platter at Herod's banquet *(see p89)*.

The Feast of Herod by Fra Filippo Lippi at Prato's Duomo

🔟 Hill Towns

Town hall, Cortona

2 Siena
MAP E4

Siena may have grown to small city size, but it retains a homey, hill-town atmosphere. Its travertine-accented brick palaces, stone towers and fabulously decorated churches are strung along three high ridges at the south end of the Chianti hills (see pp30–37 & pp94–9).

3 Volterra
MAP D4

The world's greatest alabaster craftsmen inhabit the loftiest hill town in Tuscany, whose stony medieval streets rise a cloud-scraping 555 m (1,820 ft) above the valley. This was one of the key cities in the Etruscan Dodecapolis confederation (see pp44–5 & p115). The museum (see p55) is filled with finds unearthed as the erosion that is affecting one end of town slowly exposes ancient tombs.

1 Cortona
MAP F4

This Etruscan settlement above the Chiana Valley is a trove of ancient tombs and Renaissance art. Stony buildings, steep streets and interlocked *piazze* characterize the centre. The upper town has the Sanctuary of St Margaret, the 16th-century Medici fortress and little-known lookouts (see pp42–5 & p103).

Pienza *pecorino*

4 Pienza
MAP F4

Italy's only perfectly planned Renaissance town centre was commissioned from Rossellino by Pope Pius II in the 15th century. The perimeter street offers views over the rumpled green, sheep-dotted landscape. The town's shops specialize in Tuscan wines, honey and the best *pecorino* sheep's milk cheese in all of Italy (see p121).

Montepulciano, with Tempio di San Biagio church in the foreground

7 Montalcino
MAP E4

Montalcino stands proudly high above the valley; this was Siena's last ally against Florentine rule. The hilltop eyrie is dominated by the shell of a 14th-century fortress with fantastic views, and is now a place where you can sample Montalcino's Brunello wine *(see pp70–71)*, the region's most robust red *(see p121)*.

8 Massa Marittima
MAP D4/5

The Old Town centres on a triangular piazza with the Duomo and the crenellated mayor's palazzo. The upper New Town was founded in the 14th century by the conquering Sienese, whose fortress now offers visitors sweeping hill views. The Museum of Sacred Art in the museum complex of San Pietro all'Orto holds Ambrogio Lorenzetti's *Maestà* *(see p115)*.

The clifftop town of Pitigliano

5 San Gimignano
MAP D3

The pride of this medieval Manhattan – a UNESCO World Heritage Site and the epitome of the perfect Italian hill town – are 14 stone towers of varying heights (the tallest 54 m/177 ft) that seem to sprout from the terracotta roof tiles. The town is surrounded by patchwork fields and vineyards that produce Tuscany's best DOCG white wine *(see pp24–5 & p115)*.

6 Montepulciano
MAP F4

From the Medici city gate to the hilltop Piazza Grande with its crenellated Michelozzo-designed Palazzo Comunale and brick-façaded Duomo, the main street passes *palazzi*, 19th-century cafés and wine shops where the samples of grappa and Vino Nobile *(see pp70–71)* flow freely. You can also visit the cellars beneath the town *(see p121)*.

9 Pitigliano
MAP F6

In the heart of the Alta Maremma, surrounded by valleys full of ancient tombs, Pitigliano is built upon an outcrop of tufa rock. In fact, it is difficult to tell where the cliff sides end – pockmarked as they are with cellar windows – and the walls of the houses and castle begin *(see p127)*.

10 Fiesole
MAP E2

Fiesole was the hilltop town that Roman Florentia was built to compete with. It has small archaeology and art museums, a Roman theatre, cool summertime breezes and views across to Florence *(see p89)*.

🔟 Villas and Gardens

2 Villa della Petraia

MAP E2 ▪ Via della Petraia 40 ▪ 055 452 691 ▪ Open Nov–Feb: 8:15am–4:30pm; Mar & Oct: 8:15am–5:30pm; Apr–Sep: 8:30am–4:30pm daily ▪ Closed 2nd & 3rd Mon of month, 1 Jan, 14 Aug, 25 Dec

This villa was rebuilt for Ferdinando I de' Medici by Buontalenti in 1595. Volterrano decorated the courtyard with the *Glory of the Medici* frescoes (1636–48). The English-style park is 17th-century and the terrace has panoramic views of Florence.

1 Villa Poggio a Caiano

MAP D2 ▪ Piazza de' Medici 14, Poggio a Caiano ▪ 055 877 012 ▪ Open Nov–Feb: 8:15am–4:30pm; Mar & Oct: 8:15am–5:30pm; Apr, May & Sep: 8:15am–6:30pm; Jun–Aug: 8:15am–7:30pm daily (ticket office closes 1 hour before) ▪ Adm

Giuliano da Sangallo restructured this greatest of Medici villas in 1480 for Lorenzo the Magnificent. The ballroom is a pinnacle of Mannerist painting by Pontormo, Andrea del Sarto, Filippino Lippi and Alessandro Allori. Francesco I and his second wife Bianca Cappello died here in 1587, apparently poisoned *(see p90)*.

3 Villa Vignamaggio

MAP E3 ▪ Vignamaggio, Greve ▪ 055 854 661 ▪ Open daily ▪ Adm ▪ www.vignamaggio.com

The villa's wines were, in 1404, the first to be called "Chianti" *(see p40)*. This is also where the real Mona Lisa was born (1479) and where Kenneth Branagh's *Much Ado about Nothing* (1993) was filmed. Guided tours include wine samples; a full tour includes lunch in the *enoteca*.

Villa Poggio a Caiano

Appennino sculpture, Villa Demidoff

④ Villa Demidoff

MAP E2 ▪ Pratolino ▪ 055 409 427 ▪ Open Apr, May, Sep & Oct: 10am–7pm Sat, Sun & hols (Apr–Oct: 10am–5pm Fri); Jun–Aug: 10am–8pm Sat, Sun & hols ▪ Adm

Buontalenti laid out the vast Pratolino park for Francesco I de' Medici (1568–81). The waterworks have long fallen into disrepair (the villa was demolished in 1824), but what remains is still spectacular, especially the figure of Appennino rising out of a lily pond (see p90).

⑤ Villa di Artimino "La Ferdinanda"

MAP D2 ▪ Artimino, Carmignano ▪ 055 875 141 ▪ House open by appointment

This 16th-century Buontalenti villa was built for Ferdinando I, most likely as a winter hunting lodge. Visitors can dine or spend the night here, and a wellness centre is under construction.

⑥ Villa di Castello

MAP E2 ▪ Via di Castello 47, Sesto Fiorentino ▪ 055 452 691 ▪ Open Sep–May: 9am–sunset; Jun–Aug: 8:15am–sunset daily ▪ Closed 2nd & 3rd Mon of month ▪ Adm

Cosimo I had Tribolo lay out the marvellous gardens in 1541, a combination of clipped hedges, ponds, ilex woods and statuary. The villa hosts the prestigious Accademia della Crusca, an Italian linguistics society.

⑦ Villa Reale di Marlia

MAP D2 ▪ Marlia, Capannori ▪ 0583 30 009 ▪ Open 1 Mar–2 Nov: hourly tours 10am–1pm & 2–6pm Tue–Sun (3 Nov–end Feb reservations only; Tel: 0583 30 108) ▪ Adm

This 16th-century villa was radically altered by Elisa Baciocchi to suit her 19th-century Napoleonic tastes. Only the 17th-century gardens are open.

⑧ Villa Garzoni

MAP D2 ▪ Collodi ▪ Open 8:30am–sunset daily ▪ Adm ▪ www.pinocchio.it

The villa (1633–52) is currently closed to the public, but the Renaissance and Baroque garden, set into a steep hillside, is open to visitors.

The gardens of Villa Mansi

⑨ Villa Mansi

MAP D2 ▪ Segromigno in Monte ▪ 0583 920 234 ▪ Open Nov–Mar 9am–4:30pm Mon–Fri ▪ Adm

The 16th-century statue-studded villa contains mythological frescoes painted in the late 18th century. Juvarra's Baroque gardens survive to the west side of the villa; the rest were landscaped in English style in the 19th century.

⑩ Villa Medicea di Cerreto Guidi

MAP D3 ▪ Via Ponti Medicei 12, Cerreto Guidi ▪ Closed 2nd & 3rd Mon of month, 1 Jan, 1 May, 24 & 25 Dec ▪ www.polomuseale.firenze.it/en

This villa was built in the mid-1500s as a hunting lodge for the Medici family. Today it houses the Hunting Museum and an art gallery (see p90).

🔟 Spas and Resorts

Colonnaded spa pool at Montecatini Terme

1 Montecatini Terme
MAP D2 ■ Viale Verdi 41,
Montecatini Terme ■ 0572 7781 ■
www.termemontecatini.it

A little overbuilt, but still the best place in Italy for grandiose, Liberty-style thermal establishments; drink Terme Tettuccio's waters for your digestive system, wallow in Terme Leopoldine's mud for your skin. Also take the funicular to the medieval hill town of Montecatini Alto (see p110).

2 Viareggio
MAP C2

Southernmost Riviera-style resort on the coast, a mix of grand old buildings and simple tourist hotels. The promenade is lined with restaurants and shops on one side, and a crowded but sandy beach on the other (all stretches are privately run; you pay for a chair and umbrella). Not the cleanest water, but the calm sea and sandy beach are good for children (see p109).

3 Cascate del Gorello, Saturnia
MAP E6

After Saturnia's sulphur-laden hot spring bursts out of the ground, it rushes over the Cascate del Gorello, a long slope of open-air whirlpools that form a staircase of waterfalls

and small azure pools. There, you can lie back in the warm, bubbly waters and relax for free (see p128).

4 Saturnia Spa
MAP E6 ■ 0564 600 111 ■
www.termedisaturnia.it

An elegant four-star spa, the Hotel Terme di Saturnia is built around the town's sulphur spring, whose warm waters and mineral-rich mud have long been thought to benefit the skin and respiratory system. A fitness centre is attached to the hotel, and there are also opportunities for horse riding (see p128).

⑤ Monsummano Terme
MAP D2 ▪ Via Grotta Giusti
1411 ▪ 0572 90 771

This natural sauna is formed from a series of subterranean caves that lie above a sulphurous underground lake, filled with hot mineral-laden vapours *(see p110)*.

⑥ Elba
MAP C5

Italy's third largest island offers Tuscany's best all-round coastal holiday – sandy beaches, water sports, fishing villages, resorts and vineyards. Sightseeing takes in forts, museums and mine tours devoted to the island's mineralogical wealth (discovered by the Etruscans, the iron of Elba armed the legions of Rome). There are also two villas left from the 11 months Napoleon lived here in exile *(see p127)*.

⑦ Punta Ala
MAP D5

This is little more than a modern yacht marina backed by some classy hotels. Nearby, there is riding on offer and one of Tuscany's toughest, and prettiest, golf courses amid pine groves sloping down to the sea.

⑧ Chianciano Terme
MAP F4 ▪ www.
chiancianoterme.com

It is fortunate that the spa waters of Acqua Santa clean the liver, for the historic spa town of Chianciano lies at the end of a wine road from Montalcino past the Val d'Orcia and Montepulciano. This group of thermal spas – with waters and mud

Wisteria garden, Chianciano Terme

packs to invigorate the body – is linked to the hill town of Chianciano Alto by a long string of hotels.

⑨ Monte Argentario
MAP E6

This mountainous peninsula is covered in ilex and olives, and rimmed with beaches. The trendier of its two towns is southerly Porto Ercole, where Caravaggio gasped his last. It retains a fishing village air, while Porto Santo Stefano is a slightly larger resort town and the main fishing port *(see p127)*.

⑩ Forte dei Marmi
MAP C2

One of the string of impeccable beaches along the northern Versilia, Forte dei Marmi is built around a 15th-century marble port. It stands out for its fine sands, grand ducal fort (1788) and the villas of minor nobility and the well-to-do hidden amid the pines *(see p111)*.

**A beach at
Forte dei Marmi**

TOP 10 Tuscany for Children

The Ildebranda Tomb at the Etruscan necropolis in Sovana

1 Exploring Tombs
Crawling through the ancient tunnels and tombs left by the Etruscans makes for a slightly spooky Indiana Jones-style adventure. The best are in the Maremma around Sorano, Sovana and Pitigliano *(see pp126–9)*, and near Chiusi *(p122)*.

2 Climbing the Towers and Domes
From the Duomo's dome in Florence to countless bell towers across the region, Tuscany offers youngsters dozens of fun scrambles up to dramatic lookout points, many reached only via tight, evocatively medieval sets of stairs.

3 Florence's Museo dei Ragazzi
www.museoragazzi.it
Not a place but a series of rotating workshops at the Palazzo Vecchio *(see p83)*, Museo Novecento and Museo Stibbert. Children can explore hidden parts of the Palazzo Vecchio, play with Galilean telescopes and dress up as Medici progeny.

4 Saturnia Hot Springs
Sit back and relax in a warm sulphur pool while your offspring splash and make Italian friends in this open-air slice of paradise. But keep little ones away from the upper parts of the stream where the current is very strong *(see p66 & p128)*.

5 Biking Lucca's Walls
Cycle around the top of Lucca's massive 16th-century ramparts shaded by trees, and peek down into elaborate gardens.

6 Pinocchio Park, Collodi
MAP D2 ■ Off the S435 outside Collodi ■ Open Mar–Oct: 9am–sunset daily (Nov–Feb: from 10am Sat & public holidays) ■ Adm
The hometown of *Pinocchio* author Carlo "Collodi" Lorenzini has a small themed park.

Puppet, Pinocchio Park

7 San Gimignano
The Town of Towers *(see pp24–5)* is an imposing sight: a medieval fairy-tale city full of towers to climb, alleys to explore and a half-ruined fortress

to clamber about. The torture museum stuffed with gruesome instruments appeals to children and adults alike.

8 Ludoteca Centrale, Florence

MAP P1–2 ■ **Piazza della SS Annunziata 13** ■ **Currently closed for refurbishment**

Best suited to toddlers and small children, the courtyards of Europe's oldest foundling hospital house a selection of toys. Children must be accompanied by an adult.

9 Museo Stibbert, Florence

MAP E3 ■ **Via F Stibbert 26** ■ **055 475 520** ■ **Open 10am–2pm Mon–Wed, 10am–6pm Fri–Sun** ■ **Closed 1 Jan, Easter Sun, 1 May, 15 Aug & 25 Dec** ■ **Adm** ■ **www.museostibbert.it**

Quirky private museum of armour established by Frederick Stibbert. The 16th-century Florentine weaponry is arranged as an army marching through the largest room *(see p84)*.

Exhibits at the Museo Stibbert

10 Giardino dei Tarocchi

MAP E6 ■ **Garavicchio di Capalbio** ■ **0564 895 122** ■ **Open Apr–mid-Oct: 2:30–7:30pm Mon–Sat; Nov–Mar open 1st Sat of month (free)** ■ **Adm**

This odd sculpture garden of giant Tarot card images is mosaicked with Gaudíesque coloured tile chips. Niki de Saint Phalle, the artist, sadly passed away in 2002.

TOP 10 TIPS FOR FAMILIES

Sightseeing at Florence's Duomo

1 Sightseeing Discounts
Ridotto tickets are for students and under-18s. Admission may be free for those under the ages of 6, 12 or even 18 (especially for EU citizens).

2 Try Picnicking
It's great fun, saves money, lets the children eat what they want, and gives them a break from places where they have to be on their best behaviour.

3 Order Half-Portions
A *mezza porzione* for smaller appetites costs less.

4 Share a Room
An extra bed costs at most 35 per cent more; cots and baby cribs even less.

5 Make a Base
Stay in one hotel or apartment and make day-trips. Changing hotels is a time-consuming hassle, and weekly rates are cheaper.

6 Train Discounts
Both Italo and the state railway offer discounts for families travelling together. You will save even more if you book long-distance rail travel three months in advance.

7 Rent a Car
One car is usually cheaper than four sets of train tickets.

8 Gelato Breaks
Don't overpack your itinerary. Take time to enjoy the ice cream instead.

9 Use Rest Wisely
Sightseeing is exhausting. Do as the Italians do and nap after lunch.

10 Expect to be Welcomed
Italy is a multigenerational culture, accustomed to welcoming travelling clans. And a child attempting Italian is a great icebreaker with locals.

Wine Houses

1 Antinori (Chianti)

The Antinori Marquises have been making wine since 1385, producing more than 15 million bottles annually of some of Italy's most highly ranked and consistently lauded wines. You can sample their *vini* at Florence's Cantinetta Antinori *(see p87)*.

2 Avignonesi (Montepulciano)

MAP F4 ■ **Via Colonica 1, Valiano** ■ **www.avignonesi.it**

The Falvo brothers were key in reviving the quality and raising the status of Vino Nobile in the 1990s. The huge estate also produces vintages made with Merlot and Cabernet, and one of Tuscany's finest Vin Santos. A classy showroom/free tasting bar is in Montepulciano.

3 Castello di Brolio (Chianti)

The estate that invented modern Chianti Classico is back in the Ricasoli family after years under Seagram's, and the wines have improved vastly. The "Iron Baron" Bettino Ricasoli, Italy's second prime minister, perfected the formula here in the 19th century *(see p40)*.

Bottle of Antinori wine

4 Banfi (Montalcino)

MAP E4 ■ **Call ahead for guided tours (0577 840 111)** ■ **www.castellobanfi.com**

Massive American-owned estate founded in 1978, producing scientifically perfect wines and a massive Brunello *riserva*. There's a huge shop and *enoteca* and a small glass and wine museum.

5 Monsanto (Chianti)

Full-bodied wines from the estate that was the first, in 1968, to make a single *cru* Chianti and a 100 per cent Sangiovese Chianti *(see p40)*.

6 Poggio Antico (Montalcino)

MAP E4 ■ **0577 848 044** ■ **www.poggioantico.com**

One of the least pretentious major Montalcino vineyards, this produces an award-winning velvety Brunello. They offer guided cellar tours.

7 Gattavecchi (Montepulciano)

MAP F4 ■ **Via di Collazzi 74** ■ **www.gattavecchi.com**

Top-rank Vino Nobile producer with grotto-like cellars that burrow under the adjacent church. Riserva dei Padri Serviti is their top wine. La

Vineyards at the historic Castello di Brolio estate

Cucina di Lilian offers lunchtime tasting menus pairing local produce with Gattavecchi wines and olive oil.

8 Marchesi de' Frescobaldi (Chianti Rufina/ Montalcino)

MAP E4 ▪ www.frescobaldi.it

The Frescobaldi Marquises, the largest private winemaking concern in Tuscany, have been viticulturalists for 30 generations (England's Henry VIII kept some stock on hand). They were one of the first to experiment with non-native grapes (Cabernet Sauvignon, Chardonnay, Merlot, Pinots). You can visit several estates.

Barrels at Marchesi de' Frescobaldi

9 Fonterutoli (Chianti)

Highly regarded estate in the Mazzei family since 1435, centred around a medieval village with a laid-back bar (in the *osteria*) for tippling. Vintages of the Chianti, Siepi and Brancaia have won the top Italian rankings *(see p40)*.

10 Tenuta di Capezzana (Carmignano)

MAP D3 ▪ Direct sales 10am–6pm Mon–Sat ▪ www.capezzana.it

A vineyard since 804, Capezzana single-handedly created the Carmignano DOC by adding 15 per cent Cabernet to the otherwise Sangiovese mix. They also make a rosé version called Vin Ruspo. Book ahead for tastings, or to sign up for the on-site cookery school.

TOP 10 TUSCAN WINE STYLES

Bottles of Chianti wine

1 Chianti Classico and Chianti Classico Gran Selezione
Italy's most famous reds, these are the highest quality Chiantis. Made in a region at whose heart is the original area established by Cosimo III's edict.

2 Brunello di Montalcino
One of Italy's most powerful, complex reds, Brunello is created using only the Sangiovese Grosso varietal – the wine was perfected accidentally when a blight killed all but this grape.

3 Vino Nobile di Montepulciano
Less complex, but more versatile, than Brunello. This Chianti-like blend is dominated by the Prugnolo varietal.

4 Vernaccia di San Gimignano
Tuscany's only white DOCG, a dry to semisweet pale honey elixir.

5 Sassicaia di Bolgheri
Complex, long-lived and very pricey Cabernet Sauvignon.

6 Tignanello
Antinori's complex, beefy wine made with 80 per cent Sangiovese, 15 per cent Cabernet Sauvignon and 5 per cent Cabernet Franc.

7 Chianti Rufina
This is a structured, Sangiovese-based wine from the best-known of the Chianti subzones.

8 Carmignano
One of the world's oldest official wine areas (1716), near Prato. DOCG Chianti blend with Cabernet. Balanced.

9 Morellino di Scansano
Maremma's big DOC red, 85–100 per cent Morellino (Sangiovese).

10 Vin Santo
Sweet, golden dessert wine made from raisined grapes. Aged in oak barrels.

ᴛᴏᴘ**10** Restaurants

Traditional interiors of Dorandò

1 Dorandò, San Gimignano
This elegant stone-walled restaurant keeps traditional Sangimignanese recipes alive, resurrecting superbly prepared, tasty dishes from the Middle Ages and Renaissance. They even claim that some of their dishes date back to the Etruscan era. The menu explains each in detail *(see p119)*.

2 L'Antica Scuderia, Badia a Passignano
Set amid a sea of vines beside an 11th-century abbey, this has one of Tuscany's prettiest outdoor terraces. The food is equally elegant, a refined take on Tuscan classics such as *pappa al pomodoro* (a delicious thick tomato soup) and *tagliata* (a dressed sliced steak). Black truffles feature liberally on the menu *(see p93)*.

3 Il Romito, Livorno
Spectacularly perched on a clifftop overlooking the sea, this restaurant's location is truly superb. The menu features excellent seafood dishes and good pizzas. Visitors can enjoy a drink at the bar before going on to dine on the restaurant's spacious terrace *(see p113)*.

4 Konnubio, Florence
Florence's San Lorenzo neighbourhood is experiencing a mini-renaissance, and this relaxed and friendly restaurant is the best of several recent openings. The menu is an unusual mix of traditional Tuscan and vegan dishes, occasionally on the same plate (seitan with Tuscan spices, for example). The enclosed courtyard setting and subtle lighting gives it a romantic ambience after dark *(see p87)*.

5 Antica Locanda di Sesto, near Lucca
There's been an inn here on the banks of the River Serchio between Lucca and the Garfagnana since the 1300s. Family-run for decades, the current incarnation is steeped in the cooking traditions of this mountainous corner of Tuscany. Several ingredients, including extra-virgin olive oil, are sourced fresh from the family farm. Grilled meat is a house speciality *(see p113)*.

6 La Buca di Sant'Antonio, Lucca
The best food in Lucca since 1782. Here diners will find a series of rooms hung with old kitchen implements and musical instruments. You will experience the friendliest professional welcome of any fine restaurant in Tuscany, and, of course, excellent Lucchese cooking *(see p113)*.

La Buca di Sant'Antonio in Lucca

The lovely rural trattoria La Cantinetta di Rignana

7 La Cantinetta di Rignana, near Greve in Chianti

This establishment is set amid vineyards, far from anywhere along winding dirt roads – a complete countryside trattoria experience. Curing meats hang in the doorway, and Madonna and Child icons and copper pots pepper the walls. The home-made pastas and grilled meats are delicious. There is also a glassed-in veranda for summertime dining *(see p93)*.

8 La Botte Piena, near Montefollonico

Mighty stone-and-brick walls and an oak-beamed ceiling give this place a rustic vibe. The food follows centuries-old traditions of the Sienese country-side, with the likes of hand-rolled *pici* pasta, *pecorino* cheese and *Cinta Senese* pork. The wine list is long and expertly sourced, and covers the best of Tuscany's vineyards *(see p125)*.

9 Ristorante Fiorentino, Sansepolcro

Sansepolcro's best restaurant is over 200 years old – an old-fashioned, homey, wood-ceilinged trattoria of Tuscan cuisine. The owner prefers to rhapsodize about what's best in the kitchen today rather than handing customers a menu, and enjoys discussing the works of Piero della Francesca *(see p107)*.

10 Trattoria Sant'Omobono, Pisa

Simple and traditional Pisan home cooking is offered at this hidden gem of a trattoria at the outdoor market. The menu is full of long-standing Pisan favourites such as *baccalá* (salt cod), *coniglio* (rabbit) and *brachetti alla renaiola*, an ancient recipe of pasta squares in puréed turnip greens and smoked fish *(see p113)*.

⏻ Tuscany for Free

Relaxing in the Cascate del Gorello

1 Saturnia Hot Springs
At the Cascate del Gorello *(see p66)*, you can splash in cobalt-blue pools under gentle waterfalls, as warm spring waters soak your skin in sulphur and other minerals. These open-air thermal springs are open all year round.

2 State Museum First Sundays
www.beniculturali.it/domenicalmuseo
With Italy's #DomenicalMuseo program, every state museum in Tuscany is free on the first Sunday of the month. The list includes some of the best: Florence's Uffizi *(see pp12–15)* and the Galleria dell'Accademia *(see p81)*, Piero della Francesca's frescoes in Arezzo *(see p103)* and Chiusi's Etruscan museum *(see p122)*. Arrive early to beat the queues at the major spots in Florence.

3 Tuscan Church Masterpieces
Some of Italy's most precious artworks are on show in Tuscan churches. In Pistoia, tiny Sant'Andrea *(see p53)* has Giovanni Pisano's carved stone pulpit from 1301. Pienza's cathedral *(see p59)* is one of the few that has its original gold-leaf altar-pieces still in place, rather than installed in a museum.

4 Gregorian Chant
In the church of San Miniato al Monte in Florence *(see p57)* and the Romanesque abbey of Sant'Antimo near Montalcino *(see p58)*, monks still celebrate daily prayer in chant. You can find the exact schedules at the tourist offices.

5 Florence Free Walks
www.florencefreetour.com
Free guided walks around Florence depart from outside the church of Santa Maria Novella every day. The tour in the morning focuses on Renaissance landmarks. In the afternoon, Medici rulers and their palaces take centre stage. There are no reservations or upfront charge: guides work for tips.

6 Pilgrims' Path
www.viefrancigene.org/en
The Via Francigena was the medieval pilgrims' route from Canterbury to Rome, and much of the path through Tuscany has been waymarked for 21st-century walkers. The 30-km (19-mile) stretch between San Gimignano and Monteriggioni is among the most picturesque. The website has downloadable maps.

Pilgrims' Path

7 A Village with a View
The ancient Etruscan settlement of Fiesole is ideally sited for a panorama over Florence in the valley below. A little balcony on the steep road to San Francesco monastery is the perfect spot to snap the city and Chianti hills beyond.

8 Abbazia di Monte Oliveto Maggiore
The Great Cloister at this remote monastery (see p122) has over 30 narrative panels painted by Renaissance artists Luca Signorelli and Sodoma. The drive there, through the surreal landscape of the Crete Senesi hills, is a Tuscan classic.

9 Siena's Archive Tour
Banchi di Sotto 52 ■ Visits by guided tour only at 9:30am, 10:30am & 11:30am Mon–Sat (Italian only)
From the 1250s to the beginning of the 18th century, Siena's local government commissioned illustrations for the front cover of the city ledger, often from top-rank artists like Ambrogio Lorenzetti and Sano di Pietro. You can see these "Tavolette di Biccherna" on guided visits around the Archivio di Stato or state archive (see p97).

Detail, Pontormo's *Entombment*

10 Mannerist Masterpieces
The big names of the art movement that grew around Michelangelo were all Florentines: Andrea del Sarto, Pontormo and Rosso Fiorentino. Key works are scattered around city churches and cloisters, including Santissima Annunziata (see p57), Santa Felicità and the Chiostro dello Scalzo.

TOP 10 MONEY-SAVING TIPS

Refreshing Italian gelato

1 Give heavy desserts a miss and have a much cheaper and more refreshing gelato instead.

2 When booking accommodation, don't be afraid to haggle with the hotel by email. Booking directly with them saves them commission fees.

3 At coffee bars and cafés, a *caffè al banco* (coffee had standing at the counter) costs a fraction of a *caffè al tavolo* (at the table).

4 If you are a visitor from outside the EU and are leaving the EU with the goods purchased, you can get a refund on the 22 per cent sales tax (known as IVA). Save your purchasing for one big store to hurdle the €155 lower limit for a tax refund (see p140).

5 The low season in the area runs from mid-October to March. Airfares and hotel prices drop, although coastal resorts are deserted.

6 Thursday is a popular evening for free talks at many museums, including at Florence's Strozzina. Find details at www.strozzina.org.

7 *Aperitivo* or "happy hour" buffets are unlimited from around 7 to 9pm. Buy a drink, eat your fill from the ample buffet and skip dinner.

8 Long-distance rail fares are much cheaper when booked between 90 and 120 days in advance.

9 You'll get more accommodation for your money in less attractive areas (such as around Florence's train station) or in hostels or monasteries. Look at Monastery Stays for details (see p141).

10 Eat lunch at markets frequented by locals, such as Florence's Sant'Ambrogio (www.mercatosantambrogio.it).

TOP 10 Festivals

A costumed contestant riding past the target at the Giostra del Saracino

1 Siena's Palio
MAP E4 ■ Piazza del Campo, Siena ■ 2 Jul, 16 Aug

Since the Middle Ages, Siena has staged a biannual bareback horse race around the Campo. The festivities last for a week. On the day of the race, you can stand in the centre of the Campo for free or buy a seat ticket (months in advance) from any business ringing the piazza. Enjoy the pageantry and *sbandieratori* (flag tossers), before glimpsing the furious, 90-second race.

2 Florence's Calcio Storico
MAP P4 ■ Piazza Santa Croce, Florence ■ 16–29 Jun

Football without the rules, between Florence's four traditional neighbourhoods. This violent game – with players dressed in Renaissance costume – is usually played on the dusty Piazza Santa Croce, with matches in past years taking place in Piazza della Signoria or the Boboli Gardens.

Float, Viareggio Carnevale

3 Arezzo's Giostra del Saracino
MAP F3 ■ Piazza Grande, Arezzo ■ 3rd Sun in Jun, 1st Sun in Sep

This horseback jousting contest with participants in medieval costume takes place on the sloping Piazza Grande. It's the only joust in Tuscany where the target can hit back – the "Saracen" is allowed to turn and knock the rider as he gallops past.

4 Viareggio's Carnevale
MAP C2 ■ Viale Carducci and Viale Marconi, Viareggio ■ Shrove Tue, and weekends in Lent

This carnival may lack the costumed balls of Venice, but their parade of elaborate floats is almost as famous.

5 Prato's Display of the Virgin's Girdle
MAP D2 ■ Duomo, Prato ■ Easter, 1 May, 15 Aug, 8 Sep, 25 Dec

When the Virgin was assumed, body and soul, to Heaven, Doubting Thomas was sceptical, so she handed him down her girdle as proof of her ascent. Legend has it that the girdle was eventually inherited by a Jerusalem woman who married a Prato man, who brought it to the town in the 12th century. It was later encased in a glass-and-gold reliquary, and locked in the Duomo. Five times a year the bishop shows it to crowds in the piazza and church, and lets the faithful kiss the case. A procession is then led by musicians in Renaissance-style costumes.

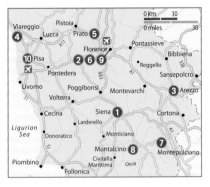

6 Florence's Scoppio del Carro

MAP M3 ▪ Piazza di S Giovanni, Florence ▪ Easter Sun

White oxen pull a firework-laden cart from the Baptistry's *Gates of Paradise* to the Duomo. During Easter mass, a mechanical dove sails on a wire down the nave and through the door to ignite the cart in an explosion of noise and colour.

7 Montepulciano's Bravio delle Botti

MAP F4 ▪ Main drag ▪ Last Sun in Aug

After a week of medieval pageantry, festivities and feasting, costumed two-man teams from the town's eight neighbourhoods prove their racing prowess by rolling hefty

Bravio delle Botti, Montepulciano

barrels up this hill town's meandering, often steep main street to the piazza at the top.

8 Montalcino's Sagra del Tordo

MAP E4 ▪ Fortezza ▪ Last weekend Oct

Montalcino celebrates hunting season by throwing a food festival in the medieval *fortezza*, roasting thousands of thrushes on spits over open fires, boiling up vats of polenta and washing it all down with region's robust Brunello wine.

9 Maggio Musicale and Estate Fiesolana

Various venues ▪ May–Aug
▪ www.maggiofiorentino.com,
www.estatefiesolana.it

May and June bring concerts, plays and recitals to Florence's theatres, churches and public spaces. From June to August, Estate Fiesolana hosts performing arts events in Fiesole; best of all are those held under the stars in the ancient Roman theatre high above the town.

10 Pisa's Gioco del Ponte

MAP C3 ▪ Ponte di Mezzo
▪ Last Sun in Jun

Pisan residents from either side of the Arno have always been rivals, and they fight it out by dressing in Renaissance costume and staging an inverse tug-of-war on Pisa's oldest bridge, trying to push a giant, leaden cart over to the other team's side.

Florence and Tuscany Area by Area

Inside the Cortile del Michelozzo in Palazzo Vecchio, Florence

TOP 10 Florence

Florence is the cradle of the Renaissance, the city of Michelangelo's *David* and Botticelli's *Birth of Venus*. It was here that the Italian language was formalized and its literature born under Dante. Here, enlightened Medici princes ruled: Lorenzo the Magnificent encouraged Michelangelo to pick up a hammer and chisel, and Cosimo II protected Galileo from the Inquisition. Today, its historic core is a UNESCO World Heritage Site. If you feel overloaded with art, explore Dante's medieval neighbourhood or the Oltrarno artisan quarter, stroll around the Boboli Gardens or venture to hilltop Fiesole *(see p89)*.

Statue, Pitti Palace

FLORENCE

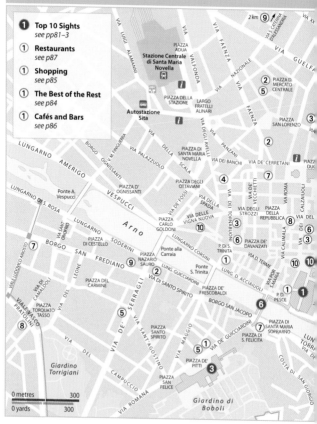

- **1** Top 10 Sights
  see pp81–3
- **1** Restaurants
  see p87
- **1** Shopping
  see p85
- **1** The Best of the Rest
  see p84
- **1** Cafés and Bars
  see p86

1 Uffizi

The greatest gallery of Renaissance art on earth, a veritable living textbook of Western art's most shining moments, showcasing masterpieces from Giotto and Botticelli through Michelangelo, Raphael and Leonardo da Vinci to Titian, Caravaggio and Rembrandt (see pp12–15).

2 The Duomo Group

Florence's religious heart: Giotto's lithe bell tower, the Baptistery's *Gates of Paradise* and Byzantine mosaics, and the Duomo museum's Michelangelo and

The beautiful Duomo buildings

Donatello sculptures – all lorded over by Brunelleschi's dome, a miracle of Renaissance engineering and architecture (see pp16–17).

3 Pitti Palace

This brawny Mannerist mansion served as Florence's royal home from 1560 until the 1860s, when Florence did a stint as Italy's capital. Backed by the beautiful, elaborate Boboli Gardens, the seven museums in the palace include the excellent Galleria Palatina of late Renaissance/early Baroque paintings (see pp18–21).

4 Galleria dell'Accademia

Michelangelo's *David* stands pensively at the end of a corridor lined by the artist's *Slaves* (see p54). The plaster casts crowding one long room hint that this is still a fine arts academy – the statues' black "pimples" are reference points to help students copy the works.

David at the Galleria dell'Accademia

THE BONFIRE OF THE VANITIES

The puritanical preacher Girolamo Savonarola took advantage of a weak Medici to seize power in 1494. The iron-fisted "Mad Monk's" reign peaked in 1497 when his bands of boys looted wealthy houses to create a giant "Bonfire of the Vanities" on Piazza della Signoria. A year later, under threat of excommunication, Florence burned Savonarola himself at the stake at the same spot as the monk's bonfire.

5 Santa Croce

Florence's "Westminster Abbey" contains the tombs of such Tuscan geniuses as Michelangelo and Galileo, as well as Giotto frescoes and a renowned leatherworking school (see p85). Off the lovely cloisters are a Renaissance chapel designed by Brunelleschi (decorated by Luca della Robbia), and a small museum with a Last Supper by Taddeo Gaddi and a Crucifix by Cimabue, restored after the infamous flood of 1966 (see p56).

6 Ponte Vecchio

MAP M4–5
■ Via Por S Maria/Via Guicciardini

The shops hanging from both sides of Taddeo Gaddi's 1345 "old bridge" have housed gold- and silversmiths since Ferdinando I evicted the butchers in the 16th century (his private corridor from the Uffizi to the Pitti passed overhead, and he

couldn't stand the smell). Even the Nazis, blowing up bridges to slow the Allied advance, found the span too beautiful to destroy and instead took down the buildings at either end.

7 San Marco

MAP N1 ■ Piazza di S Marco 1 ■ Open 8:15am–1:50pm Mon–Fri, 8:15am–4:50pm Sat & Sun; closed 2nd, 4th Mon and 1st, 3rd, 5th Sun of month ■ Adm

Cosimo il Vecchio de' Medici commissioned Michelozzo to build this Dominican monastery in 1437. This was Fra Angelico's home. He frescoed the cells of his fellow monks with devotional images and left a plethora of golden altarpieces that are now housed in the Renaissance monastery's old Pilgrim's Hospice. Fra Bartolomeo's portrait of Savonarola hangs in the "Mad Monk's" room, next to a scene of the theocrat's fiery death.

8 Il Bargello

MAP N4 ■ Via del Proconsolo 4 ■ Open 8:15am–1:50pm daily; closed 1st, 3rd, 5th Sun and 2nd, 4th Mon of month ■ Adm

Florence's sculpture gallery, installed in a medieval former town hall and prison, contains some early Michelangelos, Mannerist Giambologna's gravity-defying Flying Mercury (1564) and the city's best Donatello collection, including David in marble and David in bronze (the first nude since antiquity) and a puzzled St George (1416).

Il Pescatore at Il Bargello

Ponte Vecchio

Palazzo Vecchio's stone façade

9 Palazzo Vecchio

MAP N4 ▪ Piazza della Signoria
1 ▪ Open 9am–7pm Fri–Wed, 9am–
2pm Thu (extended hours Mon–Wed
& Fri during summer) ▪ Adm

Arnolfo di Cambio's mighty town hall
(1299–1302) is still Florence's seat of
government. Vasari, who was hired
by Cosimo I to redecorate the
medieval palace in the 1540s,
frescoed a Medici marriage around
Michelozzo's 1453 courtyard and
swathed the gargantuan Sala dei
Cinquecento with an apotheosis of
the Medici dynasty. Francesco I shut
himself away from matters of state
in his small barrel-vaulted Studiolo
to conduct scientific experiments.

10 Piazza della Signoria

MAP N4

Adjacent to the Palazzo Vecchio, the
piazza is Florence's living room and
sculpture gallery. The *Neptune* fountain by Ammannati was dismissed
by Michelangelo as a "waste of good
marble". On the palazzo's *arringheria*
– the platform from which orators
"harangued" the crowds – are copies
of Donatello's *Marzocco* (Florence's
leonine symbol) and *Judith*, and
Michelangelo's *David*. The only original, Bandinelli's 1534 *Hercules*, was
derided by Cellini as a "sack of
melons". Orcagna's 14th-century
Loggia dei Lanzi shelters Cellini's
Perseus (1545) and Giambologna's
Rape of the Sabine Women (1583).

▶ **MORNING**

Book your **Accademia** tickets
(055 294 883) *(see p81)* for 8:30am
and spend a leisurely 90 minutes
perusing the paintings and
Michelangelo statues. Next make
your way towards the **Duomo** *(see
p16–17)*. Aim to be at the **Museo
dell'Opera del Duomo** around
11am, then head to the Duomo
itself and climb the dome for
stupendous views. Pop into
the **Baptistry** for its Byzantine
mosaics and bronze doors. Stroll
down the Via dei Calzaiuoli and
turn left onto Via dei Cimatori for
lunch on-the-go from **I Fratellini**
(see p86), nibbling your sandwich
and sipping wine while lounging
on the cobbled street.

AFTERNOON

During *riposo*, trek over to the
basilica of **Santa Croce** to pay
your respects to the artistic
luminaries buried there, and
to browse the leather shop. On
your way back to the heart of
town, stop at the **Gelateria dei
Neri**, one of Florence's best
gelato parlours (Via dei Neri
9r), for a fortifying triple scoop.
Have **Uffizi** reservations *(see
pp12–15)* for 4pm: this will give
you nearly three hours to explore
before closing time. Afterwards,
stroll across the **Ponte Vecchio**
in the twilight, pause to gaze at
the Arno, then plunge into the
Oltrarno district to find a good
spot for dinner – try Pizzeria
Berberè in the Piazza de' Nerli
for Italian craft beers and some
of the best pizzas in town.

See map on pp80–81

The Best of the Rest

1 ### Churches
Florence's major churches are covered fully on pp56–7, and the Duomo on pp16–17.

2 ### Museo Archeologico
MAP P2 ■ Via della Colonna 36 ■ Open 8:30am–7pm Mon–Sat, 1st & 3rd Sun of month ■ Adm

Etruscan artifacts on display here include a silver amphora from Antioch, a wooden Hittite chariot and the Roman bronze *Idolino (see p44).*

Lion's head, Museo Archeologico

3 ### Palazzo Medici-Riccardi
MAP N2 ■ Via Cavour 3 ■ Open 9am–7pm Thu–Tue ■ Adm

A must-see in this Medici palace of 1444 are the chapel's 360° frescoes by Benozzo Gozzoli.

4 ### Casa Buonarroti
MAP P4 ■ Via Ghibellina 70 ■ Open Nov–Feb: 10am–4pm Wed–Mon (to 5pm Mar–Oct) ■ Adm

Carvings by Michelangelo are on display at his nephew's house, along with works by Baroque artists including Artemisia Gentileschi.

5 ### Casa di Dante
MAP N3 ■ Via S Margherita 1 ■ Open Apr–Sep: 10am–6pm daily (to 5pm in winter) ■ Adm

Dante is said to have been born in a house that stood here. The current building serves as a museum with displays about Dante and medieval Florence. The poet's beloved Beatrice is buried in the church across the street.

6 ### Museo Horne
MAP N5 ■ Via dei Benci 6 ■ Open 9am–2pm Thu–Tue ■ Adm

This private collection includes works by Giotto and Beccafumi.

7 ### Piazzale Michelangelo
MAP Q6 ■ Piazzale Michelangelo

Sweeping, postcard-ready panoramas of Florence.

8 ### Spedale degli Innocenti
MAP P2 ■ Piazza SS Annunziata 12 ■ Open 10am–7pm daily ■ Adm

Brunelleschi's portico is studded with terracotta foundlings by Andrea della Robbia. The Pinacoteca inside houses paintings by Piero di Cosimo, Botticelli and Ghirlandaio.

9 ### Museo Stibbert
Wacky museum renowned for its armour collections *(see p69).*

10 ### Cenacolo di Sant'Apollonia
MAP N1 ■ Via XXVII Aprile 1 ■ Open 8:15am–1:50pm (Thu & Fri: 10am–1pm); closed 1st, 3rd, 5th Sat & Sun of month, 1 Jan, 1 May & 25 Dec

This former Benedictine convent holds Andrea del Castagno's dramatic 1450 *Last Supper.* Note the turbulent marble panel behind the heads of Jesus and Judas.

Andrea del Castagno's *Last Supper*

Shopping

Ferragamo store and museum

① Ferragamo
MAP M3 ■ Via dei Tornabuoni 4r–14r ■ Open 10am–7:30pm Tue–Sat, 3:30–7:30pm Mon; museum: 10am–6pm Wed–Mon (Adm)

Flagship store and museum for designer shoes dating back to Hollywood's golden age of the 1920s.

② San Lorenzo Market
MAP M2 ■ Piazza del Mercato Centrale ■ Open 8am–8pm ■ Closed Mon Nov–Feb

This famous Florence outdoor market offers leather goods, fashion items and marbled paper. The adjacent food market is open every morning except Sunday.

③ Gucci
MAP M3 ■ Via dei Tornabuoni 10r ■ Open 10am–7pm Tue–Sat, 3–7pm Mon, 2–7pm Sun

Guccio Gucci opened a saddlery in Florence in 1904 before founding his leather-goods empire in 1921.

④ Enoteca Alessi
MAP N3 ■ Via delle Oche 27–29r ■ Open 9am–7:30pm Mon–Sat

This sweet shop's basement wine merchant is the best in town.

⑤ Pitti Mosaici
MAP L5 ■ Piazza dei Pitti 23r–24r ■ Open 9am–7pm daily ■ Closed Sun in winter

Highest-quality *pietre dure* – "mosaics" of semiprecious stones.

⑥ Emilio Pucci
MAP M3 ■ Via Tornabuoni 22r ■ Open 10am–7pm Mon–Sat

Emilio Pucci has had a fashion house in Florence for decades, offering daring prints.

⑦ Casa dei Tessuti
MAP M3 ■ Via de' Pecori 20–24r ■ Open 10am–1pm & 3–7pm Tue–Sat, 3–7pm Mon

Wonderful selection of textiles, including a few designer names. Occasional talks on Florence are held in the shop.

⑧ La Botteghina
MAP M1 ■ Via Guelfa 5r ■ Open 10am–1:30pm & 4–7:30pm Mon–Fri, 10am–1:30pm Sat

Excellent hand-painted ceramics from some of central Italy's best artisans.

La Botteghina platter

⑨ Scuola del Cuoio of Santa Croce
MAP P4 ■ Piazza di Santa Croce (inside church); on Sun enter at Via di San Giuseppe 5r ■ Open 9:30am–6pm Mon–Sat

High-quality, butter-soft leather products crafted by local artisans. All your purchases will be monogrammed in gold leaf.

⑩ Pineider
MAP L3 ■ Piazza de' Rucellai, 4/7r ■ Open 10am–7pm daily

Founded in 1774 and still family-owned, Pineider is the stationer of choice for royalty and celebrities. Their elegant handmade products include hand-engraved stationery and personalized leather goods.

See map on pp80–81

Cafés and Bars

The Pitti Gola e Cantina wine bar

1 Pitti Gola e Cantina
MAP L5 ▪ Piazza Pitti 16

A refined little wine bar with good snacks, very conveniently situated just across the square from the splendid Pitti Palace and its treasure-trove of art.

2 Il Santino
MAP L4 ▪ Via Santo Spirito 60r

On one of the Left Bank's hippest streets, this tiny wine bar serves tasty Florentine tapas plates to complement a short, but expertly chosen, wine list.

3 I Fratellini
MAP N4 ▪ Via dei Cimatori 38r

This is a traditional *fiaschetteria* – a hole-in-the-wall wine bar that also serves a range of delicious sandwiches for on-the-go street-side eating while you're out and about.

4 Beer House Club
MAP P5 ▪ Corso dei Tintori 34

This relaxed bar-pub has the biggest range of European craft beers in central Florence, with around ten rotating beers listed on the chalkboard, including brews made especially for Beer House Club.

5 Archea
MAP K5 ▪ Via de' Serragli 44

A small Belgian-style pub, this has its own microbrewery and offers thirsty customers a range of good European craft beers.

6 Cantinetta del Verrazzano
MAP N3/4 ▪ Via dei Tavolini 18–20r

Great pastries and wonderful stuffed *focaccia* sandwiches are on offer at the Cantinetta del Verrazzano, which is owned by the Chianti wine estate (*see p40*).

7 Le Volpi e l'Uva
MAP M5 ▪ Piazza dei Rossi

This establishment is a low-key, jazzy wine bar situated in the Oltrarno antiques and artisan district.

8 La Terrazza
MAP M3 ▪ Inside La Rinascente, Piazza della Repubblica

A tiny terrace café in the sky with views over Florence rooftops and the hills beyond.

9 La Cité Libreria Café
MAP K4 ▪ Borgo San Frediano 20r

A bohemian café-bookshop by day; by night a relaxed bar and eclectic events space with acoustic music.

10 Rivoire
MAP N4 ▪ Piazza della Signoria/Via Vacchereccia 4r ▪ Closed Mon

Soak up Italy in style at this classy café with tables right on the Piazza della Signoria.

Rivoire on the Piazza della Signoria

Restaurants

The stylish interior of Ora d'Aria

PRICE CATEGORIES

For a three-course meal for one with half a bottle of wine (or equivalent meal), taxes and extra charges.

€ under €35 ▪ €€ €35–70 ▪ €€€ over €70

1 Ora d'Aria
MAP M4 ▪ Via dei Georgofili 11 ▪ 055 200 1699 ▪ Closed Aug ▪ €€€

Head chef Marco Stabile cooks up creative Tuscan haute cuisine at this Michelin-starred establishment.

2 Konnubio
MAP M2 ▪ Via dei Conti 8r ▪ 055 238 1189 ▪ €

Elegant but affordable courtyard dining with Tuscan and vegan dishes on a creative menu (see p72).

3 Zeb
MAP P6 ▪ Via San Miniato 2r ▪ 055 234 2864 ▪ Closed Wed ▪ €

Informal deli café serving traditional Tuscan dishes, made daily with the freshest ingredients. The filled pastas are sublime.

4 Cantinetta Antinori
MAP L3 ▪ Piazza Antinori 3 ▪ 055 292 234 ▪ €€€

Wine bar/restaurant set within a 15th-century palazzo. The Antinori family has been making Chianti for generations, and the produce comes from their farms (see p70).

5 Sud
MAP M1/2 ▪ First floor, Mercato Centrale, Via dell'Ariento ▪ €

Florence's best pizzeria serves its pizzas in Naples style, with doughy crusts and thin bases. The menu is short with only authentic choices such as the Margherita.

6 Da Tito
Via San Gallo 112r ▪ 055 472 475 ▪ Closed Sun ▪ €

Theatrical and genuine, this popular neighbourhood trattoria is a traditional taste of old Florence.

7 iO: Osteria Personale
MAP J4 ▪ Borgo San Frediano 167r ▪ 055 933 1341 ▪ Dinner only, closed Sun & Aug ▪ €€

Hipster vibe, contemporary cooking. Expect classic Tuscan produce like octopus or *Cinta Senese* pork.

Sorbet at iO: Osteria Personale

8 Alla Vecchia Bettola
MAP J5 ▪ Viale Vasco Pratolini 3/7 ▪ 055 224 158 ▪ Closed Sun & Mon; 2 weeks in Aug ▪ €€

Old-fashioned dishes – some, such as *testicciole* (stew in a halved sheep skull), not for the weak of stomach.

9 Il Pizzaiuolo
MAP Q4 ▪ Via dei Macci 113r ▪ 055 241 171 ▪ Closed Sun ▪ €

Crowded pizza parlour also serving tasty Neapolitan pasta dishes. Expect a wait even with reservations.

10 Brac
MAP N5 ▪ Via dei Vagellai 18r ▪ 055 094 4877 ▪ Closed Aug ▪ €

Florence's best informal vegetarian and vegan restaurant, with counter seating and a romantic courtyard.

See map on pp80–81 ←

TOP 10 Around Florence

The lush hills and wide Arno Valley spreading out from Florence are overlooked by most travellers making a beeline for Siena and Pisa. Skip the main roads and discover the spots known only to locals. There's no lovelier route to Siena than the S222 Chiantigiana through the famed terracotta centre Impruneta to the castle-topped, vine-clad hills of the Chianti wine region. Just off the road to Pisa, the towns of Prato and Pistoia would be better known for their rich heritages of Romanesque architecture and Renaissance art were they not overshadowed by their mighty neighbours. Villas built by the Medici dot the countryside northwest of town.

Sculpture, Roman theatre, Fiesole

AROUND FLORENCE

0 kilometres   10
0 miles   10

Barberino di Mugello · ⑥ · Scarperia · S302
Vaiano · San Piero a Sieve · ⑥ Borgo San Lorenzo
④ ⑦ Pistoia · Montale · Vicchio
Agliana · S325 · Vaglia · Bivigliano · Dicomano · S551
⑤ · A1 · Pratolino · ⑦ Villa Demidoff
③ Prato · Sesto Fiorentino · Rufina
④ ⑦ ⑧ ⑧
Quarrata · A11 · ② Fiesole · Pontassieve
Villa Poggio a Caiano ⑨ · Campi Bisenzio · Florence · Arno
Vinci ⑤ · Artimino ② · Signa · Arno · Bagno a Ripoli
Montelupo Fiorentino · S67 · Scandicci · Galluzzo · Rignano sull'Arno · S69
Empoli · Certosa del Galluzzo ⑧ · A1 · ③ Leccio
FI-PI-LI · Pesa · Reggello
Ponte a Elsa · Cerbaia · ⑩ Impruneta
San Casciano in Val di Pesa · Incisa in Val d'Arno
Elsa · S429 · Montespertoli · RA3 · Greve · Figline Valdarno · S69
Castelfiorentino · Tavernelle Val di Pesa · ① ③ · Greve in Chianti
⑨ · Panzano in Chianti
① · ⑥ ⑨ ⑩ · Cavriglia
San Donato · ① Chianti · S408
S429 · Radda in Chianti ⑤ · ②
Poggibonsi · ⑩ Castellina in Chianti

① **Top 10 Sights**
see pp89–91

① **Restaurants**
see p93

① **Shops and Cafés**
see p92

Vineyards stretching to the horizon in the Chianti region of Tuscany

1 Chianti

Tuscany's famous wine region has vineyards and castles, market towns and monasteries *(see pp38–41).*

2 Fiesole

MAP E2 ■ Tourist office: Via Portigiani Zenobi 3 ■ 055 596 1323

This hilltop Etruscan settlement is a short ride from Florence on a No. 7 bus. The 11th-century cathedral was assembled using ancient Roman columns, and houses Renaissance sculptures by Giovanni della Robbia and Mino da Fiesole. The remains of a Roman theatre and baths are still used for Estate Fiesolana summer concerts. The steep road up to San Francesco church, with its quiet cloisters and quirky missionary museum, passes a popular park, shaded by ilex and peppered with watercolourists reproducing its famous view of Florence *(see p61).*

3 Prato

MAP D2 ■ Tourist office: Piazza Buonamici 7 ■ 0574 24 112
■ www.pratoturismo.it

The mercantile tradition of this fast-growing city dates to 15th-century financial genius Francesco Datini, famed "Merchant of Prato" and inventor of the promissory note. His frescoed palazzo is one of the best preserved of its kind in Italy. Prato's finest art decorates the Duomo *(see p59)*, but the Galleria Comunale has a lovely collection of early Renaissance polyptych altarpieces by such masters as Filippo Lippi and Bernardo Daddi. The half-ruined Castello dell'Imperatore (1420s), its ramparts and grassy interior now a city park, was built by Emperor Frederick II to defend the road from his German kingdom to his lands in southern Italy.

4 Pistoia

MAP D2 ■ Tourist office: Piazza Duomo 4 ■ 0573 21 622
■ www.turismo.pistoia.it

An ancient Roman town of metalworkers – the industry's thin daggers, which evolved into hand-guns, were called *pistole* after the city. It is an artistic crossroads where the striking Romanesque stripes in San Giovanni Fuoricivitas and the Duomo *(see p59)* meet the Florentine Renaissance glazed terracottas festooning the Ospedale del Ceppo. Gothic art comes in the form of colourful 1372 frescoes covering the Cappella del Tau, and a Giovanni Pisano carved pulpit (1298–1301) in the church of Sant'Andrea.

Aerial view of the Duomo, Pistoia

An aerial view of the medieval hill town of Vinci

5 Vinci
MAP D2 ■ **Tourist office:**
Via della Torre 11 ■ **0571 568 012**

In 1452, on the outskirts of this unassuming medieval hill town, an illegitimate child was born named Leonardo; he grew up to become one of the greatest scientific minds and artistic talents in history. The 11th-century Castello Guidi now houses a Museo Vinciano devoted to over 100 models of the master's inventions. Up the road, set in an olive-clad farmscape that might have come straight from one of his works, is Leonardo's simple *casa natale* (birthplace).

6 Borgo San Lorenzo
MAP E2 ■ **Tourist office:**
Piazzale Lavacchini 1/"Pro Loco" Via O Bandini 6
■ **055 845 6230**

The medieval capital of the Mugello region is surrounded by Medici villas such as Villa Medicea di Cerreto Guidi *(see p65)* and the Michelozzo-designed Castello del Trebbio (1461). In the town, painstakingly rebuilt after a 1919 earthquake, the 12th-century Pieve di San Lorenzo church contains Renaissance altarpieces by Taddeo Gaddi and Bachiacca, a damaged *Madonna* fresco by Giotto and apse murals by local Art Nouveau ceramics entrepreneur Galileo Chini (1906).

Statue, Pieve di San Lorenzo

7 Villa Demidoff
The original Villa di Pratolino and its park were commissioned by Francesco I for his mistress, Bianca Cappello, and served as the setting for their wedding in 1579. The villa is gone, but Bernardo Buontalenti's fountain-filled and statue-studded Pratolino park remains a favourite excursion from Florence *(see p65)*.

8 Certosa del Galluzzo
MAP E3 ■ **Galluzzo** ■ **Open for guided tours only 9–11am & 3–4pm Tue–Sun (until 5pm in summer)**

Originally established in 1341, this charterhouse was home to Carthusian monks from its founding to 1956. It now serves monks of the Cistercian Order. The building retains an original small monk's church, a visitable cell and peaceful Renaissance cloisters set with della Robbia terracotta *tondi* and a small gallery of the Pontormo frescoes dating from 1523–5.

9 Villa Poggio a Caiano
This ultimate Renaissance Medici villa was designed by Giuliano da Sangallo at the end of the 15th century for Lorenzo the Magnificent. Until this point, country houses were fortified, with rooms facing an inner courtyard. Sangallo's design was revolutionary, with rooms overlooking the

FLORENTINE EXPANSION

In 1125, Florence virtually obliterated its hilltop neighbour Fiesole and began to prowl for land. It allied with the amenable (Prato, 1351), conquered the recalcitrant (Pistoia, 1301; Pisa, 1406) and built the rest (Livorno, 1571). Three years of bloody battle finally defeated Siena (1554–7), and in 1569, the Medici pope Pius V named Cosimo I de' Medici the Grand Duke of Tuscany.

countryside and a central hall with frescoes by such masters as Filippino Lippi and Pontormo *(see p64)*.

⑩ Impruneta

MAP E3 ■ Tourist office: **Piazza Garibaldi/ "Pro Impruneta"** ■ 055 231 3729

This terracotta-producing town is famed for its Renaissance collegiate church of Santa Maria. Flanking the high altar are chapels designed by Michelozzo and decorated with Luca della Robbia terracottas. The one on the right contains a fragment of the True Cross, the left an icon of the Virgin (supposedly painted by St Luke), buried here during the early Christian persecutions and dug up when the church foundations were laid. Also on view are fine Baroque paintings and a Mannerist crucifix by Giambologna.

Santa Maria church, Impruneta

A TOUR OF THE REGION

▶ MORNING

Start with **Pistoia** *(see p89)* and the stupendous Gothic frescoes inside Capella del Tau (incredibly, a private owner in the 16th century whitewashed over them). Go down to zebra-striped San Giovanni Fuoricivitas for a Romanesque feast.

It's a short walk to Pistoia's octagonal Baptistry, designed (maybe) by Andrea Pisano and unmistakable with its hoops of green and white marble. Don't dawdle: you need time for the **Duomo** opposite (closes at 12:30, *see p59*) then Sant'Andrea (closes 12:30). Head back to the centre by way of the Ospedale del Ceppo and its colourful glazed terracotta frieze. Eat lunch at long-standing local favourite **La BotteGaia** *(see p93)* just off the picturesque market square where medieval-style second storeys project over the ground floors of the buildings.

AFTERNOON

From Pistoia, it's a quick drive to **Prato** *(see p89)*. Stop first at Palazzo Datini's frescoes (the St Christopher by the door was a common feature, believed to help protect those leaving the house) to pay your respects to the medieval "Merchant of Prato", who inscribed his account ledgers "For God and Profit".

Visit the **Duomo** *(see p59)* and, if you have the time, the adjacent Museo dell'Opera del Duomo and the Palazzo Pretorio. Grab a bag of *cantucci* (biscuits) at Antonio Mattei and clamber onto the broken ramparts of Castello dell'Imperatore for views of Santa Maria delle Carceri (1485–1506), a fine High Renaissance church.

See map on p88 ⬅

Shops and Cafés

Antica Macelleria Falorni

1 Antica Macelleria Falorni, Greve

MAP E3 ■ Piazza Matteotti 69–71

The ceilings at this butcher's have been hung with prosciutto and the walls festooned with salami since 1729. Good wines, too *(see p38)*.

2 Ceramiche Rampini, near Radda

MAP E3 ■ Casa Beretone di Vistarenni (road to Siena)

One of the best Italian ceramicists, producing classy and whimsical designs. You can buy anything from a single piece to a full dinner service.

3 The Mall, Leccio Regello, near Florence

MAP E3 ■ Via Europa 8 (take Incisa exit from A1)

Come here for savings on clothes, shoes and accessories by names such as Armani, Gucci, St Laurent and Bottega Veneta. The outlet centre runs a shuttle bus from Florence (055 865 7775 Mon–Fri for bookings). The modern building is well signposted and is 3 miles (5 km) off the main road.

4 Antonio Mattei, Prato

MAP D2 ■ Via Ricasoli 20–22

Since 1858, this shop has been making the best *cantucci* (biscuits) in Italy. Buy some to take back home, along with a bottle of Vin Santo.

5 Luciano Porciatti, Radda

MAP E3 ■ Piazza IV Novembre 1–3

Excellent deli with fine cheeses and meats. The nearby grocer sells wine and packaged regional foods.

6 Barberino Designer Outlet, Barberino di Mugello

MAP E2 ■ Via Meucci ■ Closed Mon Feb–May, Oct, Nov

Over 100 designer outlets as well as several cafés and eateries.

7 Luca Mannori, Prato

MAP E2 ■ Via Lazzerini 2

Delicious cakes and a huge variety of chocolates are sold at this pastry shop and chocolate-makers.

Sweet treats at Luca Mannori

8 Nuovo Mondo, Prato

MAP E2 ■ Via Garibaldi 23

Stop by for delicious sweets, panini and pastries with classy service if you find yourself in this busy shopping street.

9 Verso x Verso, Panzano

MAP E3 ■ Via Giovanni da Verrazano 17

A modern showroom selling traditional leather goods. Jackets, bags and shoes made to measure.

10 Accademia del Buon Gusto, Panzano

MAP E3 ■ Piazza Ricasoli

There's nowhere quite like Stefano Salvadori's *enoteca* if you want to get schooled in the wines of the Chianti.

Restaurants

1 **La Cantinetta di Rignana, near Greve**
MAP E3 ▪ Loc Rignana ▪ 055 852 601 ▪ Closed Tue ▪ €€

Deep in the countryside, set among vineyards, this is the ultimate in rural feasting: both the setting and the food are second to none (see p73).

2 **Da Delfina, Artimino**
MAP D2 ▪ Via della Chiesa 1 ▪ 055 871 8074 ▪ Closed Mon; Sun dinner (in winter) ▪ Payment with some cards accepted ▪ €€

This is one of Tuscany's finest countryside restaurants, mixing classy service with refined but traditional cooking. *Coniglio con olive e pinoli*, rabbit with olives and pine nuts, is a speciality.

3 **Enoteca Ristorante Gallo Nero, Greve in Chianti**
MAP E3 ▪ Via Battisti 9 ▪ 055 853 734 ▪ Closed Thu ▪ €€€

A wide selection of meat dishes, home-made pastas and a good wine list are offered at this friendly, family-run restaurant.

4 **La BotteGaia, Pistoia**
MAP D2 ▪ Via del Lastrone 17 ▪ 0573 365 602 ▪ Closed Mon ▪ €

This long-standing local favourite is a traditional Slow Food *osteria* serving the cuisine of northern Tuscany.

5 **La Fontana, Prato**
MAP D2 ▪ Via di Canneto 1 ▪ 0574 27 282 ▪ €€

Specializes in simple, authentic Tuscan food with a variety of fragrant home-baked desserts. Portions are generous and prices reasonable.

6 **Oltre il Giardino, Panzano**
MAP E3 ▪ Piazza G Bucciarelli 42 ▪ 055 852 828 ▪ €€

Enjoy generous portions, intimacy and picture-postcard views. The menu changes daily. Advance booking is advised.

PRICE CATEGORIES
For a three-course meal for one with half a bottle of wine (or equivalent meal), taxes and extra charges.
....
€ under €35   €€ €35–70   €€€ over €70

7 **Trattoria dell'Abbondanza, Pistoia**
MAP D2 ▪ Via dell'Abbondanza 10 ▪ 0573 368 037 ▪ Closed Wed ▪ €

Cosy eatery behind Piazza del Duomo serving superb Tuscan fare. Try the glazed figs.

8 **Baghino, Prato**
MAP D2 ▪ Via dell'Accademia 9 ▪ 0574 27 920 ▪ €€€

Tuscan and Italian dishes at the best restaurant in the historic town centre.

9 **L'Antica Scuderia**
MAP E3 ▪ Via Badia a Passignano 17, Badia a Passignano ▪ 055 807 1623 ▪ Closed Tue ▪ €€

Classic Tuscan dining amid an ocean of Chianti vines (see p72).

10 **Albergaccio, Castellina**
MAP E3 ▪ Via Fiorentina 63 ▪ 0577 741 042 ▪ Closed Sun ▪ €€

A creative, nouvelle touch is given to refined Tuscan dishes, such as ricotta gnocchi under shaved black truffles and thyme.

Elegant interiors of Albergaccio

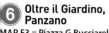*See map on p88*

TOP 10 Siena

Siena offers the sunny disposition of a Gothic brick-built hill town to contrast with historic rival Florence's stately Renaissance marble. Founded by the Etruscans, Siena developed during the Middle Ages in part due to the Via Francigena pilgrim route that passed through the town. As a thriving medieval merchant and textile town, Siena produced a colourful, courtly Gothic school of painting as well as a building boom, but it all came to a crashing halt when the Black Death of 1348 decimated the population. Florence dominated thereafter, but luckily for today's visitors this means that, aside from a few Baroque churches, Siena lacked the funds to overhaul its look – its exquisite medieval core is now a UNESCO World Heritage Site.

Siena's Duomo

SIENA

Siena's beautiful Piazza del Campo

1 Piazza del Campo

Siena's half-moon of a public square is one of the loveliest *piazze* in all of Italy, so rich in sightseeing opportunities that it counts as one of the area's unmissable sights (see pp34–5). Its broad slope is home to the biannual Palio horse race (see

p76) as well as daily streams of strollers, coffee-drinkers, readers and picnickers.

2 Palazzo Pubblico

Piazza del Campo
■ Open 10am–6pm daily ■ Adm

Siena's medieval town hall is a genteel brick palace. The rooms were so gorgeously decorated with early 14th-century art – including Simone Martini's *Maestà* and Ambrogio Lorenzetti's incomparable *Allegory of Good and Bad Government* – that they've been turned into the Museo Civico (see p36).

3 Duomo

Piazza del Duomo
■ Open daily ■ Adm

This massive Gothic cathedral complex, another unmissable sight (see pp30–32), is filled with art by Michelangelo, Pisano, Pinturicchio, Bernini, Duccio and Donatello.

4 Pinacoteca Nazionale

The Pinacoteca (see p55) boasts a comprehensive collection of Sienese painting (though the master-pieces of the school are housed else-where). Seek out the 14th-century Madonnas by Simone Martini and Pietro Lorenzetti, admire Ambrogio Lorenzetti's *Annunciation* or compare Beccafumi's cartoons (full-sized preparatory sketches on *cartone*, or "large paper") for the Duomo's floor panels and his Mannerist *Christ Descending into Limbo* to his rival Sodoma's High Renaissance works.

Detail of Lorenzetti's *Annunciation*

ST CATHERINE OF SIENA

Italy's patron saint Caterina Benincasa (1347–80) put on a nun's veil (though she never took vows) after her first vision of Christ at the age of 8; she received the stigmata at 28. Her wisdom won her the ambassadorship of Florence to Pope Gregory XI in Avignon in 1376, where she worked to convince the pope to bring back the papacy to Rome. In 1970, she became the first female Doctor of the Church.

---

5 Santa Maria della Scala
Piazza del Duomo
■ Open 10:30am–7pm ■ Adm
■ www.santamariadellascala.com

This former hospital, which operated from the 9th century to the 1990s, is being restored and transformed into one of Europe's largest cultural centres. Visitors can tour the oratories, chapels, the church and museums. Several spaces host changing exhibitions. Don't miss the Renaissance frescoes in the Sala del Pellegrino, which depict scenes of hospital life not too different from today – a monkish surgeon doctoring an injured leg, another taking a urine sample, a third dozing as his patient describes symptoms *(see p32)*.

6 San Domenico
Piazza S Domenico

This massive, architecturally uninspired brick church of 1226 contains a portrait of St Catherine by her contemporary and friend Andrea Vanni. The saint's mummified head and thumb are revered in a chapel decorated with frescoes on her life

by Sodoma (1526) and Francesco Vanni. Matteo di Giovanni executed the saintly transept altarpieces.

7 Enoteca Italiana
Fortezza Medicea ■ Open noon–8pm Mon, noon–1am Tue–Sat

The vaulted cellars of the massive 16th-century Medici fortress host Italy's national wine museum. It's far from comprehensive though, since vintners send in cases on a voluntary basis. Everything is for sale, and you can sample Italy's oenological bounty by the glass at small tables inside or outside on the terrace.

8 Via Banchi di Sopra
Via Banchi di Sopra

Siena's main *passeggiata* street for evening promenading is lined with palaces. Until Palazzo Pubblico was finished, the city council met in the piazza between San Cristofano church and the 13th-century Palazzo Tolomei, now a bank. Up the street, Piazza Salimbeni is flanked by the Renaissance Palazzo Tantucci and Palazzo Spannocchi and the Gothic Palazzo Salimbeni. Together, this group of buildings houses Monte dei Paschi di Siena, the world's oldest bank (established 1472) and city's chief employer, and its small, worthy collection of Sienese paintings.

9 Casa di Santa Caterina
Costa di Sant'Antonio 6
■ Open 9am–12:30pm & 3–7pm daily

The house in which the saint was born was made a sanctuary in 1466, with a modest Baroque church that contains the

San Domenico church

Frescoes, Casa di Santa Caterina

12th-century Pisan Crucifixion that gave Catherine the stigmata, a brick loggia (built in 1533 by Baldassare Peruzzi) and a small oratory with Baroque paintings by Francesco Vanni, Il Riccio and Il Pomarancio. Follow the staircase past Catherine's cell to see if the Oratorio dell'Oca and its frescoes of angels are open.

Ledger cover detail, Archivio di Stato

⑩ Archivio di Stato
Banchi di Sotto 52 ▪ Visits by guided tour only at 9:30am, 10:30am, 11:30am Mon–Sat (Italian only)

Siena's state archive houses city accounts going back as far as 1258, which may not sound gripping, until you find out that the Sienese were in the habit of commissioning major local artists to decorate the cover of their annual accounts ledger. This unique collection of "Tavolette di Biccherna", housed in the archive museum, holds charming miniature masterpieces by Francesco di Giorgio, Ambrogio Lorenzetti, Beccafumi and others (see p75).

A DAY IN SIENA

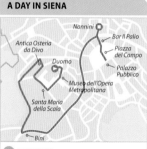

▶ MORNING

Start with the **Duomo** group (see p95), especially if it's winter, as the museum closes in the afternoon. Explore the Gothic nooks and Baroque crannies of the cathedral itself first, then pop across to **Santa Maria della Scala**. Don't skip the **Museo dell' Opera Metropolitana** (see p32) with works by Giovanni Pisano, Donatello and Duccio, plus fabulous views from the façade wall. Finally, descend the stairs to see the Baptistry before heading back around the other side of the Duomo for lunch at **Antica Osteria da Divo** (see p99). Skip dessert so that you can pick it up at the **Bini** pastry shop, located a quick 5-minute walk away at Via Stalloreggi 91–93, but don't eat it just yet.

AFTERNOON

Stroll back up Via Stalloreggi and Via di Città, where there are plenty of attractive shops, on your way to the **Piazza del Campo** (see p95). Either eat your Bini pastries or grab an outdoor table at **Bar Il Palio** (Piazza del Campo 47–9). Order a coffee or glass of wine, and drink in the ambience of one of the loveliest squares in Italy. Then head inside the **Palazzo Pubblico** (see p95) for the **Museo Civico** (see p36), which displays Siena's greatest Gothic art. Exit the Campo on the north side to join the locals for an espresso or Campari at the famed café **Nannini** (see p98) before joining the lively evening *passeggiata* (stroll) on Via Banchi di Sopra.

See map on pp94–5 ◀

Shops, Cafés and Wine Bars

① Nannini
Via Banchi di Sopra 22–4

Siena's renowned premier café roasts its own coffee and serves delicious pastries.

② Ceramiche Artistiche Santa Caterina
Via di Città 51 and 74–6 ▪ 10am–8pm daily

Franca, Marcello and son Fabio produce Siena's best ceramics. The black, white and "burnt sienna" designs are based on the Duomo's floor panels.

Ceramiche Artstiche Santa Caterina

③ Tessuti a Mano
Via San Pietro 7 ▪ 10am–1pm & 1:30–7pm Mon–Fri, 1:30–5pm Sat

Fioretta Bacci works her giant looms at the back, turning out colourful, unique knitwear.

④ Cortecci
Via Banchi di Sopra 27 and Il Campo 30–31 ▪ 9:30am–7:30pm Tue–Sun

Men's and women's designer fashion (Armani, Gucci, Prada, Versace) as well as some lesser-known, more affordable labels.

Designer fashion at Cortecci

⑤ Antica Drogheria Manganelli
Via di Città 71–3 ▪ 7:30am–7:30pm Mon–Sat

Speciality Sienese foods, such as wines, preserves, cheeses, salamis and biscuits, are sold in a well-preserved 1879 shop.

⑥ Siena Ricama
Via di Città 61 ▪ 9:30am–1pm & 2:30–7pm Mon–Fri, 9:30am–1pm Sat

Bruna Fontani's exquisite embroidery and needlepoint is inspired by medieval Sienese art, from illuminated manuscripts to Lorenzetti frescoes.

⑦ Il Papiro
Via di Città 37 ▪ 9:30am–7:30pm daily

Chain of stationery stores specializing in marbled paper and leather-bound blank books.

⑧ Compagnia dei Vinattieri
Via delle Terme 79 ▪ 0577 236 568

Innovative dishes are coupled with old favourites like *pici cacio e pepe* (pasta with *pecorino* and black pepper) at this tiny *enoteca*. Wines are its strength. Don't miss the cellar in a medieval aqueduct.

⑨ Aloe & Wolf Gallery
Via del Porrione 23 ▪ 10:30am–1:30pm & 3–7:30pm Mon–Sat

This shop tucked behind Piazza del Campo sells vintage clothing and art.

⑩ Louis Ciocchetti
Via Banchi di Sopra 91 ▪ 10am–7pm daily

Jewellery, watches and Etruscan reproduction jewellery – all made in Italy – are for sale here.

Restaurants

Enjoying a meal at Osteria Le Logge

① Osteria Le Logge
Via del Porrione 33 ■ 0577 48
013 ■ Closed Sun ■ €€

This ancient converted pharmacy offers the best traditional cuisine and friendliest service in town.

② Antica Osteria da Divo
Via Franciosa 29 ■ 0577 286
054 ■ Closed Tue ■ €€

Medieval ambience, easy-going service and modern Tuscan cooking – including an Italian trend of pairing each main course with a side dish.

③ Castelvecchio
Via di Castelvecchio 65 ■ 0577
47 093 ■ Closed Tue, Sun (occasion- ally open for lunch) ■ €

The creative Tuscan food is quite refined for the price at this intimate little place. There is a daily selection of vegetarian meals.

④ Grotta di Santa Caterina "da Bagoga"
Via della Galluzza 26 ■ 0577 282 208
■ Closed Sun dinner & Mon ■ €

Run by a former Palio jockey, this cellar-like restaurant specializes in traditional Sienese dishes such as stuffed chicken and wild boar stew.

⑤ Tre Cristi
Vicolo di Provenzano 1 ■ 0577
280 608 ■ Mon–Sat ■ €€

A bastion of the Siena restaurant scene, this charming, traditional trattoria has a focus on fish.

⑥ Antica Trattoria Papei
Piazza del Mercato 6 ■ 0577
280 894 ■ €

Large, family-run trattoria serving solid Tuscan dishes under beamed ceilings (avoid the modern room to the right), or on the piazza outside.

⑦ Gino Cacino di Angelo
Piazza del Mercato 31 ■ 0577
223 076 ■ Open 7:30am–8pm daily ■ €

Sandwiches and cold cuts available to eat in or take away. The owner is fanatical about sourcing the best local ingredients.

⑧ La Taverna del Capitano
Via del Capitano 6–8
■ 0577 288 094 ■ Open 12:30–3pm & 7:30–10pm daily ■ €

A hand-scribbled menu of hearty dishes, with laid-back service and funky modern art.

⑨ La Sosta di Violante
Via Pantaneto 115 ■ 0577 43
774 ■ Closed Sun ■ €

There is plenty of meat on the menu at this friendly, modern *osteria* named after a Bavarian princess. An extensive wine list complements the food.

⑩ Osteria La Chiacchera
Costa di Sant' Antonio 4 ■ 0577
280 631 ■ €

Remarkably cheap and no cover charge. The *cucina povera* ("poor people's cuisine") and the great desserts change daily.

See map on pp94–5 ←

Eastern Tuscany

Etruscan statue, Cortona

Arezzo province stretches from the thickly forested mountains of the Casentino in the north, down the northern arm of the Arno River valley, past the hamlet of Caprese where Michelangelo was born, to the wide Chiana Valley, the regional breadbasket. Aside from the happenstance of Michelangelo's birthplace, artistically the province is dominated by two early Renaissance titans: Sansepolcro's own Piero della Francesca in the province's northern half, and, in the south, the Cortona-born Luca Signorelli (1441–1523), whose fresco technique Michelangelo later studied avidly.

EASTERN TUSCANY

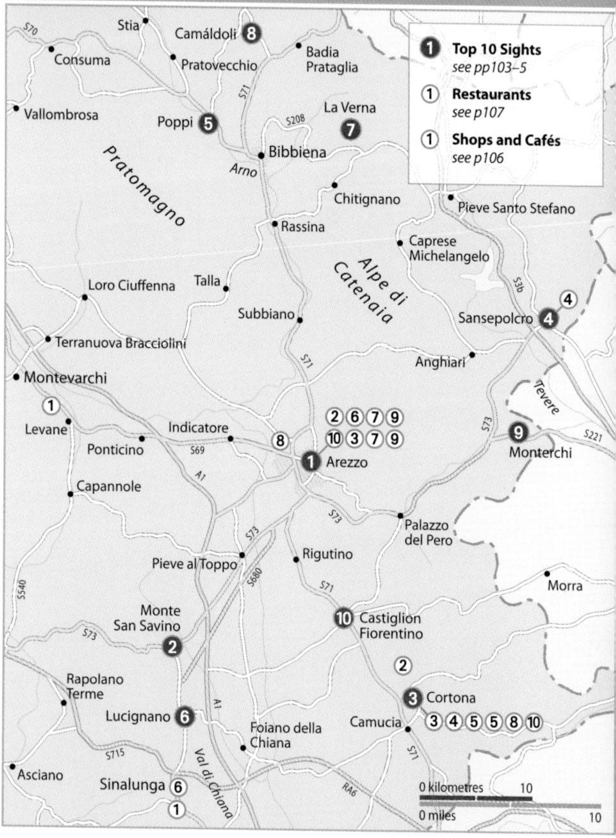

①	**Top 10 Sights** see pp103–5
①	**Restaurants** see p107
①	**Shops and Cafés** see p106

Previous pages Countryside around Pienza, Southern Tuscany

Heraldic shields at Arezzo's Piazza Grande during the Giostra del Saracino

① Arezzo
MAP F3 ▪ Tourist office: Piazza della Repubblica 28 ▪ 0575 377 678 ▪ arezzo.intoscana.it

An Etruscan city, then a Roman pottery centre, Arezzo was later home to Guido Monaco, who was the inventor of modern musical notation in the 11th century; the poet Petrarch (1304–74), and Giorgio Vasari (1512–74), architect and author of the first art history text, *Lives of the Artists*. The broad, sloping Piazza Grande is the setting for the town's Giostra del Saracino *(see p76)*. The bell tower, façade and medieval Calendar reliefs of the 12th-century Santa Maria della Pieve are in Lombard-Romanesque style, but the Pietro Lorenzetti altar-piece (1320) is pure Sienese Gothic. Arezzo's Duomo has some excellent stained-glass windows by French master Guillaume de Marcillat, and a fresco by Piero della Francesca. The 14th-century San Francesco *(see p59)* is graced with Piero's restored fresco cycle *Legend of the True Cross*.

② Monte San Savino
MAP F4 ▪ Tourist office: Piazza Gamurrini 3 ▪ 0575 849 418

This ceramics town has a small pottery museum and the Santa Chiara church, which contains early works in terracotta by native sculptor Andrea Sansovino (1460–1529). He also carved marble (a sarcophagus in the Pieve), designed the loggias and cloisters of Sant'Agostino and collaborated with architect Antonio da Sangallo the Elder on the Loggia dei Mercanti, opposite Sangallo's lovely Palazzo di Monte.

③ Cortona
The quintessential Tuscan hill town, Cortona has Etruscan tombs, medieval alleys, Renaissance art and excellent restaurants *(see pp42–5)*.

④ Sansepolcro
MAP F3 ▪ Tourist office: Via Matteotti 8 ▪ 0575 740 536

This medieval town has a reputation built around home-grown genius Piero della Francesca *(see p53)*. The Museo Civico *(see p54)* – alongside works by Signorelli and natives Santi di Tito and Raffaellino del Colle – has Piero's *Madonna della Misericordia*, the *San Giuliano* fresco fragment and the compelling *Resurrection*.

Detail, Piero's *Resurrection of Christ*

The hill town of Poppi

7 La Verna

MAP F3 ▪ Santuario della Verna ▪ 0575 5341 ▪ Open 6:30am–7:30pm daily (10pm summer)

St Francis himself founded this clifftop monastery. A Baroque frescoed corridor passes the now-enclosed cave where he slept. At the end of the corridor is the Cappella delle Stimmate, built over the site where the saint received his stigmata in 1224. For a sense of the saint's La Verna, unencumbered by buildings, walk to Sasso Spico, a rocky outcrop where the holy man prayed.

5 Poppi

MAP F3

The sweetest Casentino hill town, this is dominated by the Castello dei Conti Guidi (1274–1300), built by Lapo and Arnolfo di Cambio (also the architect of Florence's Palazzo Vecchio). Inside is a chapel, frescoed by 14th-century artist Taddeo Gaddi.

6 Lucignano

MAP F4

This tiny, elliptical town has a single street, which spirals to the lovely 16th-century Collegiata church. Behind the church, the Palazzo Comunale houses a museum with late Gothic Sienese paintings and a 2m- (6ft-) high gold reliquary dubbed *Tree of Lucignano* (1350–1471).

8 Camáldoli

MAP F2 ▪ Vie Eremo 5, Camáldoli ▪ 0575 556 012 ▪ Open winter 9am–1pm & 2:30–7pm daily; summer 9am–1pm & 2:30–7:30pm daily ▪ www.camaldoli.it

San Romualdo established this Benedictine community in 1012, although the monastery is 15th century and the Vasari-decorated church 16th. 1.6 km (1 mile) up a forest path lies the secluded hermitage (only men are admitted), a tiny village of monkish cottages alongside a Baroque church.

9 Monterchi's Madonna del Parto

MAP F3 ▪ Museo della Madonna del Parto, Via della Reglia 1 ▪ 0575 70 713 ▪ Open 9am–1pm & 2–7pm (to 5pm Oct–Mar) Wed–Mon ▪ Adm

Piero della Francesca's masterwork has the unusual subject of a heavily pregnant Virgin Mary, her tired face

---

ST FRANCIS OF ASSISI

Son of a wealthy Assisi merchant, Francis (1182–1226) gave up his carousing, soldiering way of life after a crucifixion image spoke to him with an instruction to "rebuild my church". He renounced worldly goods, wrote delightful poems and preached poverty and charity – the foundation of the Franciscan Orders. In 1224, while praying on La Verna, he received history's very first stigmata.

Monterchi's *Madonna del Parto*

and drooping eyes revealed by angels pulling back the curtains. It was painted in a nearby chapel, where it became a focus of pilgrimage for pregnant women until it was moved to this small museum.

⑩ Castiglion Fiorentino
MAP F4 ▪ Tourist info: Piazza Risorgimento 19 ▪ 0575 658 278

Off the Piazza del Municipio and its lovely 1513 Vasari loggia stands the Pinacoteca. Housed in the former church of St Angelo, its trove of art includes the 13th-century *St Francis* by Margarito d'Arezzo, a fragment of Gaddi's *Maestà* (c.1328) and *St Francis Receiving the Stigmata* (c.1486) by Bartolomeo della Gatta.

Vasari loggia, Castiglion Fiorentino

A DAY IN AREZZO

▶ MORNING

Start at the **Museo Archeologico Mecenate** (Via Margaritone 10), a museum of corallino pottery and other ancient artifacts that stands on a former Roman amphitheatre. Then head up Corso Italia to the **Piazza Grande** for coffee at one of the cafés under Vasari's loggia. Admire the square's Gothic and Renaissance *palazzi* before visiting the church of **Santa Maria della Pieve**. Then continue on Italia, turn left onto Vicolo dell'Orto to climb up past the **Casa di Petrarca** (the poet's supposed house), then turn right onto Via Andrea Cesalpino to arrive at the **Duomo** and its masterful stained glass. Afterwards, stop by the tiny **Museo del Duomo** to see paintings by Tuscan artists Bartolomeo della Gatta and the father and son duo Spinello and Parri Aretino. Then wander back downhill to lunch at **Gastronomia Il Cervo** *(see p107)*.

AFTERNOON

Having prebooked, head for the Piero works in **San Francesco** *(see p59)*. Return to Corso Italia to grab a gelato from **Cremi** *(see p106)*, then walk back down Via Cavour to the **Badia delle Sante Flora e Lucilla**. Above the altar note the trompe l'oeil "dome" (1702) painted by Baroque master of illusion Andrea Pozzo. Then walk down Via Garibaldi past SS Annunziata to the **Casa di Vasari** (Via XX Settembre 55), home of historian and Medici court painter Giorgio Vasari. End at nearby **San Domenico**, which has a Cimabue crucifix carved in the 1260s.

See map on p102

Shops and Cafés

1 Prada Outlet, Montevarchi
MAP E3 ▪ Levanella (S69)
▪ 055 91 96528

Arrive early in the day to avoid missing out on some incredible deals on high fashion in this back-of-a-factory complex just off the A1.

2 Milly Bar, Arezzo
MAP F3 ▪ Corso Italia 102
▪ 3927 477 054

The lovely terrace is the main draw here. The panini and cocktails for *aperitivo* are recommended.

3 Caffé degli Artisti, Cortona
MAP F4 ▪ Via Nazionale 18
▪ Open Tue–Sun

Part locals' bar, part tourist shop selling honey, preserves, biscuits, meats, spices and olive oils.

4 L'Antico Cocciaio, Cortona
MAP F4 ▪ Via Benedetti 24

A lovely pottery shop selling ceramics in a traditional palette of yellow, green and cream. Many patterns feature daisies (a design first used by Gino Severini).

5 Antica Drogheria, Cortona
MAP F2 ▪ Via Nazionale 3
▪ Open 9am–1pm & 3–8pm

Boutique stuffed with wines, grappa and the health products of the Camáldolesi monks.

6 Gelataria Artigianale Cremì, Arezzo
MAP F3 ▪ Corso Italia 100

Central Arezzo's best natural gelato, offering creative and classic flavours like *fiordilatte* (milk). The small outlet also sells frozen yogurt.

Stalls at Arezzo's Antiques Market

7 Arezzo's Antiques Market
MAP F3 ▪ Piazza Grande
▪ Open 7:30am–3pm 1st weekend of month

Italy's top monthly antiques market. Over 600 dealers crowd the Piazza Grande and streets around it.

8 Uno A Erre, Arezzo
MAP F3 ▪ Via Fiorentina 550, Strada Statale di Val d'Arno
▪ Open Mon–Sat

You can buy gold jewellery direct from this world-renowned manufacturer.

Ceramic plate, L'Antico Cocciaio

9 Macelleria Aligi Barelli, Arezzo
MAP F3 ▪ Via della Chimera 22b

Famous local butcher specializing in meats (mainly salami) from the Casentino region. Perfect for picnics.

10 Sotto San Francesco, Arezzo
MAP F3 ▪ Via di S Francesco 5

A plethora of wines, olive oils and local artisan products, including Aghiari lace, Monte San Savino ceramics and wrought iron.

Restaurants

PRICE CATEGORIES
For a three-course meal for one with half a bottle of wine (or equivalent meal), taxes and extra charges.
....
€ under €35   €€ €35–70   €€€ over €70

① Locanda dell'Amorosa, Amorosa

MAP F4 ▪ Near Sinalunga ▪ 0577 677 211 ▪ www.amorosa.it ▪ Closed Mon ▪ €€€

A 14th-century farm complex and inn, with a refined restaurant in the converted stalls. Classy Tuscan cuisine is served in a rustic, fire-warmed setting. Booking advised.

② Il Falconiere, Cortona

MAP F4 ▪ San Martino in Bocena 370 (just north of Cortona) ▪ 0575 612 927 ▪ €€

The *limonaia* of Silvia and Riccardo Baracchi's 17th-century estate now houses this Michelin-starred restaurant, one of the finest in the region, adding rich flourishes to the already excellent Tuscan cuisine.

③ Gastronomia Il Cervo, Arezzo

MAP F3 ▪ Via Cavour 38 ▪ 0575 20 872 ▪ Closed Mon ▪ €

There's a regular menu here, but the best choices are whatever's fresh at the deli counter downstairs, including seasonal salads and handmade fresh pasta dishes.

④ Ristorante Fiorentino, Sansepolcro

MAP F3 ▪ Via L Pacioli 60 ▪ 0575 742 033 ▪ Closed Wed ▪ €

Old-fashioned inn serving hearty, traditional food (see p73).

⑤ Preludio, Cortona

MAP F4 ▪ Via Guelfa 11 ▪ 0575 630 104 ▪ Closed Mon ▪ €

This gastronomic destination in Cortona serves nouvelle Tuscan dishes in a Renaissance palazzo setting (the frescoes are modern).

⑥ Il Forcillo

MAP F4 ▪ Viale Gramsci 7 ▪ 0577 630 102 ▪ Closed Mon and lunch Tue & Sun ▪ €€

At this Tuscan *osteria*, annexed to a lovely hotel, there is a wide choice of local cuisine served by friendly staff. Try the ravioli with cheese and nettle.

⑦ Paperi e Civette, Arezzo

MAP F3 ▪ Piazza San Gemignano 1 ▪ 0575 300 801 ▪ Closed Mon ▪ €

Elegant dining room offering several modern combinations, like pasta with salmon and a mojito to drink.

⑧ La Grotta, Cortona

MAP F4 ▪ Piazza Baldelli 3 ▪ 0575 630 271 ▪ Closed Tue ▪ €

Outdoor seating on a tiny piazza, stony medieval rooms and solid Tuscan dishes make this popular with locals and college students.

⑨ Antica Osteria l'Agania, Arezzo

MAP F3 ▪ Via Mazzini 10 ▪ 0575 295 381 ▪ Closed Mon ▪ €

Cosy trattoria where the comfort food includes *grifi e polenta* (fatty veal stomach in polenta).

⑩ La Locanda nel Loggiato, Cortona

MAP F4 ▪ Piazza di Pescheria 3 ▪ 0575 630 575 ▪ Closed Wed ▪ €

Diners come here to enjoy the balcony setting and sample the delicious Tuscan cuisine made from quality local produce.

Tables at La Locanda nel Loggiato

See map on p102

TOP10 Northwestern Tuscany

The coastal northwestern corner of Tuscany is a land of craggy mountains, wide plains and beautiful Romanesque architecture. Proud, independent Lucca, with its bicycling grandmothers and exquisite Renaissance sculpture, managed to stay a Medici-free republic until Napoleon invaded. Lively university city Pisa retains its cultural heritage of the 11th to the 13th centuries, when its navy ruled the Western Mediterranean. Its magnificent medieval Campo dei Miracoli is now a UNESCO World Heritage Site. Brash upstart Livorno has grown exponentially since the 16th century to become a major port. The three cities still nurse long-held bitter rivalries.

Bust of David, Carrara

AREA MAP OF NORTHWESTERN TUSCANY

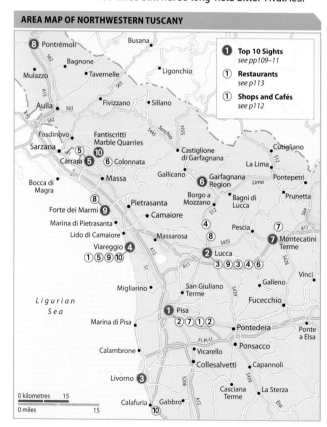

	Top 10 Sights see pp109–11
	Restaurants see p113
	Shops and Cafés see p112

1 Pisa
A favourite day trip of visitors to Tuscany, offers more than just a leaning tower. The city's gorgeous collection of Romanesque buildings called the "Field of Miracles" is among Tuscany's top sights *(see pp26–9)*.

2 Lucca
Another of the region's top sights, Lucca is a small, elegant city of avid cyclists, church concerts, Romanesque façades and exquisite Renaissance sculpture *(see pp46–7)*.

3 Livorno
MAP C3 ▪ Tourist office: Via Alessandro Pieroni 18/20 ▪ 0586 894 236 ▪ www.comune.livorno.it

Although Florence had already subjugated Pisa in the 16th century, Pisa's silty harbour and unsure loyalties prompted Cosimo I to hire Buontalenti to build him a new port from scratch. Livorno and Pisa have been traditional rivals ever since. Livorno is Tuscany's second city, but short on sights when compared with Pisa. There is just Pietro Tacca's Mannerist masterpiece *Monumento ai Quattro Mori* (1623–6) at the port, the somewhat wishfully named Venezia Nuova (New Venice) canal district, built by partly dismantling Buontalenti's Fortezza Nuova, and the Museo Civico Giovanni Fattori. The last is devoted to native son Fattori, one of the leading artists of the 19th-century Macchiaioli (Tuscan "Impressionists"). Artist Amedeo Modigliani was also born here (but worked in Paris), as was composer Pietro Mascagni.

Carnevale parade, Viareggio

4 Viareggio
MAP C2 ▪ Tourist office: Viale Carducci 10 ▪ 0584 962 233 ▪ www.luccaturismo.it

Of all the Versilia beach resorts, Viareggio has the most style and substance. The Liberty style (Art Nouveau) of its many villas, cafés and buildings harks back to the resort's heyday in the 1920s. Its Carnevale parade *(see p76)*, along the popular palm-shaded seafront promenade Viale G Carducci, is renowned throughout Italy.

Fortezza Nuova, Livorno

The Ponte del Diavolo spanning the Serchio in the Garfagnana

⑤ Carrara

MAP C2 ■ Tourist office: Piazza 2 Giugno 1 ■ 0585 641 471

Carrara is a quarry town, its snowy white marble the source of grandiose sculpture from ancient Rome to Michelangelo to Henry Moore. The town's Duomo is pure Carrara marble, and marble-cutting shops and sculptors' studios fill the streets. On the main square, look for the plaque and relief of stone-carving tools that mark the house where Michelangelo once stayed. The Museo del Marmo features the ancient Roman altar Edicola di Fantiscritti.

⑥ Garfagnana Region

MAP C2–D2 ■ Tourist office: Lucca (see p47)

The Serchio River valley north of Lucca's plain is bounded on the west by the Apuan Alps, which are home to the Grotta del Vento (Cave of the Winds). To the east are the wilds of the Garfagnana Mountains. Stopping points in the region include Borgo a Mozzano, which consists of an inn and the Ponte del Diavolo bridge. Legend has it that this was built by the Devil in exchange for the first soul to cross it (villagers sent a dog). Today virtually forgotten, in the

1930s Montecatini Terme poster

19th century Bagni di Lucca was one of Europe's most fashionable spas, visited by all the English Romantic poets. Europe's first licensed public casino opened here in 1837. Barga's white Duomo has a marvellously detailed 13th-century pulpit carved by Guido da Como. The Este dukes once owned the 14th-century fortress of Castelnuovo di Garfagnana, and installed poet Ludovico Ariosto as commander and toll-taker.

⑦ Montecatini Terme

MAP D2 ■ Tourist office: Viale Verdi 66 ■ 0572 772 244

This posh, if overbuilt, thermal spa town is worth staying in to experience one of the 19th-century Grande Dame hotels. Above the town, medieval Montecatini Alto is a favourite escape for its cool summer breezes and a cappuccino on the piazza, while nearby Monsummano Terme (see p67) has the attraction of natural cave saunas.

⑧ Pontrémoli

MAP B1 ■ Museum: Castello di Piagnaro ■ 0187 831 439 ■ Open Oct–May: Tue–Sun; Jun–Sep: daily ■ Adm

Stranded up a northern spit of Tuscany is Pontrémoli and its

GIACOMO PUCCINI

The operatic composer (1858–1924) was born in Lucca at Corte San Lorenzo 9. A small museum here includes the piano that Puccini used to compose *Turandot*. He wrote his masterpieces *La Bohème*, *Tosca* and *Madame Butterfly* (and also hunted ducks) at his villa on the shores of Lake Massaciuccoli. The villa is also now a museum.

Museo delle Statue-Stele. Some of the museum's 20-odd prehistoric menhirs (large upright stone slabs) date from 3000 BC, the more elaborate ones from 200 BC.

⑨ Forte dei Marmi
MAP C2 ■ Tourist office:
Via C. Spinetti 1 ■ 0584 280 253

A tiny resort favoured by jet-setters, this village is set back amid the pine forest, its beach lined with colourful little beach cabanas.

⑩ Fantiscritti Marble Quarries
MAP C2 ■ 9am–dusk daily

Featured in the opening scenes of Bond film *Quantum of Solace*, these marble quarries make the Apuan Alps above Carrara appear snow-capped year round. Fantiscritti has a museum of traditional stonecutting tools, which can be reached by following the Carrione River to the Vara Bridge, a former rail link to the docks that was converted to road use in 1965.

Marble quarries at Fantiscritti

PISA AND LUCCA IN A DAY

▶ MORNING

Start your day at **Pisa's** "Field of Miracles" *(see p109)*. Admire the Pisano pulpits in the Duomo *(see p58)* and the perfect acoustics of the Baptistry. Then compare the artist's original sketches with reproductions of the finished frescoes at the Museo delle Sinopie across the piazza. Admire the cathedral's treasures at the Museo dell'Opera del Duomo near the Leaning Tower, where charts show how the Campo buildings form various perfect geometries. Then take a bus or taxi south to Pisa's great but oft-missed sight, the excellent painting collection at the Museo San Matteo. Stroll back along the Arno to the Ponte di Mezzo, turn right up Borgo Stretto then left into the colourful Vettovaglie Market to lunch at the **Trattoria Sant'Omobono** *(see p113)*.

AFTERNOON

Catch a train or drive to **Lucca** *(see pp46–7)*, where your first stop is the Duomo *(see p58)*. A 5-minute walk north will take you to Torre Guinigi, well worth climbing for the panoramas. Walk another few minutes north through Piazza Anfiteatro and under the glittering façade of San Frediano to see its *Miracles of San Frediano* frescoes and the shrunken body of St Zita, patron saint of maids and ladies-in-waiting. Retrace your steps to fashionable Via Fillungo, then walk south to the impressive San Michele in Foro. To end your day, head to the city walls. If you are staying the night, rent a bike to ride along the top of the walls (the shops close at 7:30pm but you can return it the next day); if not, stroll the walls on foot.

See map on p108 ←

Shops and Cafés

Arturo Pasquinucci, Pisa
MAP C3 ▪ Via Oberdan 22

Treat yourself – or a (very good) friend – to a present from this 1870 shop, selling classy Italian kitchenware ranging from contemporary porcelain to Alessi gadgets.

Caffè dell'Ussero, Pisa
MAP C3 ▪ Lungarno Pacinotti 26 ▪ No credit cards

Look out over the Arno River and imbibe with the ghosts of Pisa's intellectual élite at one of Italy's oldest literary cafés, opened in 1794.

 Carli, Lucca
MAP C2 ▪ Via Fillungo 95

This atmospheric antique jewellers set under frescoed vaults dates from 1800 and also sells watches.

Enoteca Vanni, Lucca
MAP C2 ▪ Piazza Salvatore 7

Lucca's best wine shop is guaranteed to raise the hairs on your neck, with its hundreds of bottles crowded into small cellar rooms.

Gran Caffè Margherita, Viareggio
MAP C2 ▪ Viale Margherita 30

A late Art Nouveau version of an Oriental palace, this historic bar is also a restaurant and is in a fantastic location on Viareggio's main shopping street.

Gran Caffè Margherita, Viareggio

Forisportam, Lucca
MAP C2 ▪ Piazza S Maria Bianca 2

This is another good shop for buying presents and souvenirs; you'll pay decent prices for highly decorated Renaissance-style ceramics from Montelupo and Deruta.

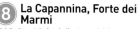 Caffè Kosì, Montecatini Alto
MAP D2 ▪ Piazza G Giusti 1

Set in a pretty medieval town above Montecatini Terme, this has been a popular café since 1878. Allow sufficient time to sample the dozens of cocktails and exotic fruit gelato.

La Capannina, Forte dei Marmi
MAP C2 ▪ Viale della Repubblica 16

Since 1929 La Capannina – part cocktail bar/restaurant and part nightclub – has been serving the best beachside refreshments around in this upmarket area.

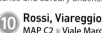 Bar Galliano, Viareggio
MAP C2 ▪ Viale Marconi 127

This historic café in the heart of the seaside promenade's shopping district is well known for its excellent ice creams, as well as great coffee, cakes and savoury snacks.

Rossi, Viareggio
MAP C2 ▪ Viale Margherita 50/ Viale Marconi 16

Rossi has been in the same family for five generations. They sell elegant pieces from the top names in Italian jewellery design for the discerning customer. Their Viale Marconi boutique carries fashionable gold and silver adornments for the younger set. Rossi also sells silver and watches.

Restaurants

Romano at Viareggio

PRICE CATEGORIES

For a three-course meal for one with half a bottle of wine (or equivalent meal), taxes and extra charges.
....
€ under €35   €€ €35–70   €€€ over €70

① Romano, Viareggio
MAP C2 ▪ Via Mazzini 122 ▪ 0584 31 382 ▪ Closed Mon; Jan; Tue lunch in summer ▪ €€

Run by the Franceschini family, this is among the town's good seafood restaurants. Excellent wine list.

② Trattoria Sant'Omobono, Pisa
MAP C3 ▪ Piazza Sant'Omobono 6 ▪ 050 540 847 ▪ Closed Sun dinner ▪ €

Classic trattoria in the market area specializing in traditional Pisan cooking such as baccalà or salt cod and other seafood *(see p73)*.

③ La Buca di Sant'Antonio, Lucca
MAP C2 ▪ Via della Cervia 3 ▪ 0583 55 881 ▪ Closed Sun dinner, Mon ▪ €

The ambience, classy but friendly service and superlative food make this a great choice *(see p72)*.

④ Antica Locanda di Sesto, near Lucca
MAP C2 ▪ Via Ludovica 1660 ▪ 0583 578 181 ▪ Closed Sat ▪ €€

There has been an inn here since the 1300s. Family-run place, with ingredients such as extra virgin olive oil fresh from the family farm *(see p72)*.

⑤ Ristorante Ninan, Carrara
MAP C2 ▪ Via Bartolini 3 ▪ 0585 74 449 ▪ €€

Tiny but comfortable wine bar and trattoria, where the chefs have

trained with the best in the business. The restaurat serves up some superb local seafood.

⑥ Venanzio, Colonnata, near Carrara
MAP C2 ▪ Piazza Palestro 3 ▪ 0585 758 033 ▪ Closed Sun dinner, Thu; Christmas–Jan ▪ €€

Venanzio Vannucci produces his own *lardo di Colonnata* (herbed pork lard). Also try the ravioli with mountain herbs and guinea fowl with truffles.

⑦ Osteria dei Cavalieri, Pisa
MAP C3 ▪ Via San Frediano 16 ▪ 050 580 858 ▪ Closed Sat lunch, Sun ▪ €

A friendly tavern on the ground floor of a medieval tower-house. Try the beans and *funghi* (mushrooms).

⑧ Ristorante Butterfly, Marlia, near Lucca
MAP C2 ▪ SS12 del Brennero 192 ▪ 0583 307 573 ▪ Open dinner daily, Sun lunch; closed Wed ▪ €€€

This Michelin-starred restaurant serves creative Italian cuisine from several regions.

⑨ Da Leo, Lucca
MAP C2 ▪ Via Tegrimi 1 ▪ 0583 492 236 ▪ No credit cards ▪ €

Da Leo is crowded with locals and buzzing with conversation. Try the *zuppa ai cinque cereali*, a soup filled with grains and legumes.

⑩ Il Romito, Livorno
MAP C3 ▪ Via del Litorale 274, Antignano ▪ 0586 580 520 ▪ Closed Oct–May: Wed, plus 2 weeks in Jan ▪ €€

Spectacular clifftop setting and fresh fish on the menu *(see p72)*.

See map on p108

TOP10 Western Hill Towns

Ceramic plate, Massa Marittima

When people imagine the archetypal Tuscan hill town, they are most likely to be picturing those in the area west of Siena. This is where San Gimignano – one of Tuscany's seven UNESCO World Heritage Sites – thrusts its grey stone towers into blue skies, where Volterra's medieval streets and alabaster artisans sit atop "a towering great bluff that gets all the winds and sees all the world" (D H Lawrence). More off the beaten track, the underrated Elsa Valley is home to other attractive hill towns, including Colle di Val d'Elsa, Certaldo and Castelfiorentino, which have virtually no crowds and offer a better glimpse of genuine Tuscan town life.

WESTERN HILL TOWNS

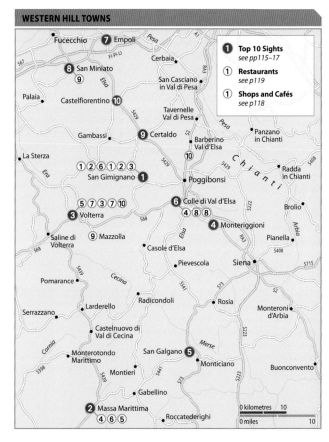

1 Top 10 Sights
see pp115–17

1 Restaurants
see p119

1 Shops and Cafés
see p118

The charming medieval hill town of Volterra

1 San Gimignano

The ultimate hill town ranks second to none among Tuscany's most unmissable sights for its fine white wine, gorgeous Gothic frescoes and remarkable medieval stone "skyscrapers" (see pp24–5).

2 Massa Marittima

MAP D4 ■ Tourist office: **Via Todini 5** ■ **0566 906 554** ■ **www.turismomassamarittima.it** ■ **0566 902 289**

This old mining town has a number of esoteric museums on the subject. In the lower Old Town, the Dark Ages reliefs on the Romanesque Duomo (see p58) are worth a look. The Palazzo del Podestà, once the seat of the mayor, dates to the early 13th century. The upper New Town has the Gothic Torre del Candeliere and ramparts, with fine views over the town and Colline Metallifere (literally the "iron-rich hills"). The Museum of Sacred Art in the San Pietro all'Orto complex holds Ambrogio Lorenzetti's *Maestà* (1330s) and a tiny pre-Etruscan menhir, a flat stone carved vaguely as a person (see p61).

3 Volterra

MAP D4 ■ Tourist office: **Piazza dei Priori 20** ■ **0588 87 257** ■ **www.volterratur.it**

Alabaster-carving is the speciality of this windswept town (see p60). The Museo Etrusco Guarnacci (see p55) has one of Italy's finest Etruscan collections, and the worn basalt heads adorning Porta all'Arco (4th century BC) represent Etruscan gods. The remains of Roman baths and a theatre are best seen from the viewing point off Via Guarnacci. The Pisan-striped 13th-century Duomo, with its meticulously carved and painted ceiling, houses a host of Byzantine and Renaissance treasures, while the Pinacoteca boasts a fully intact Taddeo di Bartolo altarpiece (1411), Ghirlandaio's final painting *Apotheosis of Christ* (1492), Luca Signorelli's *Annunciation* (1491) and Rosso Fiorentino's masterful early Mannerist *Deposition* (1521).

4 Monteriggioni

MAP E4 ■ Tourist office: **Piazza Roma** ■ **0577 304 834**

The subject of the most popular aerial-shot postcard in Tuscany is a tiny hamlet two streets wide. It is entirely enclosed within medieval walls, whose 14 towers are compared by Dante to the Titans guarding the lowest level of Hell. The town holds a week-long medieval festival every year in July.

An aerial view of Monteriggioni

Atmospheric San Galgano abbey

⑤ San Galgano
MAP E4 ■ Abbazia di S Galgano ■ Open 9am–sunset ■ Adm

This roofless 13th-century abbey and unique domed chapel on the hillside above are associated with the legend of a 12th-century soldier who plunged his sword into a stone to mark the end of his warrior ways. Ambrogio Lorenzetti frescoes (1344) illustrate the holy vision that triggered the incident (see p33).

⑥ Colle di Val d'Elsa
MAP E3 ■ Tourist office: Via del Castello 33 ■ 0577 922 791

Enter from the west to pass under Baccio d'Agnolo's Mannerist Palazzo Campana gate (1539). The Duomo features a Giambologna/Pietro Tacca bronze crucifix and a nail said to be from Christ's cross. The archaeological museum in the Palazzo Pretorio is interesting for the 1920s political graffiti scrawled on this former prison's walls by imprisoned Communists. The sgraffito-covered façade of Palazzo dei Priori hides a small museum of Sienese paintings.

⑦ Empoli
MAP D3 ■ Tourist office: c/o Empoli Glass Museum, Via Ridolfi 70 ■ 0571 76 714

Piazza Farinata degli Uberti is ringed by 12th- and 13th-century palaces and the Romanesque Sant'Andrea church. The Museo della Collegiata di Sant'Andrea contains a 1425 *Pietà* painted by Masolino da Panicale and a 1447 font carved by Bernardo Rossellino. Masolino shows up again at the church of Santo Stefano with a large *Madonna and Child* fresco; Rossellino with an *Annunciation*.

⑧ San Miniato
MAP D3 ■ Tourist office: Piazza del Popolo 1 ■ 0571 42 745

Frederick II built the imposing hilltop "Rocca" (fortress) when this was the Tuscan stronghold of the German Holy Roman Emperors. The Duomo's (rebuilt) Romanesque brick façade is studded with 13th-century North African majolica bowls.

⑨ Certaldo
MAP D3 ■ Tourist office: Piazzetta del Vicariato 3 ■ 0571 656 721

In this charming little brick town, Renaissance artists Benozzo Gozzoli and Giusto d'Andrea teamed up to work on the *Giustiziati* tabernacle in the former church of SS Thomas e

Colle di Val d'Elsa

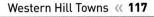

Frescoes, Palazzo Pretorio, Certaldo

Prospero, which is now part of the Palazzo Pretorio museum complex. Inside SS Michele e Jacopo church, a 1503 bust and 1954 tombstone commemorate *Decameron* author Boccaccio (1313–75), who may have been born in Certaldo; the Casa del Boccaccio, in which he passed his final years, is now a small museum.

⑩ Castelfiorentino
MAP D3 ▪ Tourist office: Via Ridolfi 13 ▪ 0571 629 049 ▪ Closed mid-Oct–Mar: pm & Sun

Santa Verdiana is the loveliest and most celebrated Baroque church in Tuscany. Its interior is swathed in frescoes depicting the odd life of Verdiana, who walled herself into a cell here for 34 years with two snakes, sent by God to test her.

DANTE

Dante Alighieri (1265–1321) was Florence's White Guelph (papal) diplomat to San Gimignano. Exiled from Florence on trumped-up charges when the Black Guelphs took over, Dante roamed Italy writing poetry, including the epic *Divine Comedy*. His choice of writing in Tuscan vernacular rather than Latin legitimized and codified the Italian language.

▶ **MORNING**

Begin early in the morning in **Volterra** *(see p115)*, starting with San Francesco and its amazing *Legend of the True Cross* frescoes. On the Piazza dei Priori, admire the Palazzo dei Priori (1208–57) inside and out. It is the oldest Gothic town hall in Tuscany and was the model for most others, including Florence's Palazzo Vecchio. Tucked into an alcove on the square is the back door of the Duomo – dive inside. Afterwards, pause for coffee and a pastry at L'Incontro *(see p118)*, then head back to the piazza and down Via dei Sarti to the Pinacoteca and Fiorentino's *Deposition (see p52)*, a Florentine Mannerist masterpiece. The museum is usually blissfully quiet. Continue on this street into Via di Sotto, which is lined with good alabaster workshops, then to Via Don Minzoni for the Museo Etrusco Guarnacci *(see p55)*.

AFTERNOON

Drive 8 km (5 miles) to the pretty hamlet of **Mazzolla** for a rustic lunch at the Trattoria Albana *(see p119)* before driving another 28 km (17 miles) to **San Gimignano** *(see pp24–5)*. You should get there just as the tour buses are leaving (but before 4pm in winter, when things close early). Admire the Collegiata frescoes before clambering up the Torre Grossa for one of Tuscany's most beautiful panoramas over the surrounding hills and vineyards. If you have time after descending – and after pausing at the Museo Civico – head to the other end of town for Sant'Agostino's Benozzo Gozzoli frescoes (before 6:30pm). Try to be back up at the ruined Rocca for sunset over the towers.

See map on p114 ←

Shops and Cafés

Gelato and sorbet at the Gelateria "di Piazza", San Gimignano

1 Gelateria "di Piazza", San Gimignano

MAP D3 ▪ Piazza della Cisterna 4

It's well worth queuing for the best gelato and sorbet in town, made by Sergio in unusual flavours such as pink grapefruit and sparkling wine.

2 Souvenir Shops, San Gimignano

MAP D3 ▪ Via S Giovanni

Tacky souvenir shops line the Via S Giovanni, selling medieval-style crossbows, swords and flails of varying degrees of realism. Most of them are small and very blunt, but some are fully functional.

3 Società Cooperativa Artieri Alabastro, Volterra

MAP D4 ▪ Piazza dei Priori 4–5

Since 1895 this has been the main outlet for alabaster artisans without a shop of their own.

4 Manufactum, Colle Val d'Elsa

MAP E3 ▪ Via del Castello 32

Colourful Tuscan ceramics made and hand-painted in the shop.

5 Enoteca Le Logge, Massa Marittima

MAP D4 ▪ Piazza Garibaldi 11

Great, simple Old World café with tables set under the partly frescoed portico of the piazza; their gelato and sandwiches are worth a try.

6 Enoteca la Botte e il Frantoio, San Gimignano

MAP D3 ▪ Via S Giovanni 56

This retail outlet for Luciano Bruni's Vernaccia wine also sells a range of olive oils and other top wines from across Tuscany.

7 L'Incontro, Volterra

MAP D4 ▪ Via Matteotti 18

This pastry and panini wine bar occupies an airy vaulted medieval room. Don't miss the artisan gelato sold out front.

8 Belli, Colle di Val d'Elsa

MAP E3 ▪ Via Diaz 10

The Etruscans once crafted crystal in this area. Belli is the best of those workshops in this region carrying on the tradition, producing both refined objects and souvenirs.

9 Il Cantuccio di Federigo, San Miniato

MAP D3 ▪ Via P Maioli 67

The Gazzarrinis have been making superb pastries, cakes and biscuits for five generations. To go with their delicious *cantucci* they carry over 40 Vin Santo labels.

10 Spartaco Montagnani, Volterra

MAP D4 ▪ Via Porta all'Arco 6

Take time to visit the shop of this local sculptor who creates original bronzes as well as replicas of works in the museum.

Restaurants

PRICE CATEGORIES
For a three-course meal for one with half a bottle of wine (or equivalent meal), taxes and extra charges.
....
€ under €35   €€ €35–70   €€€ over €70

1 Dorandò, San Gimignano
MAP D3 ▪ Vicolo dell'Oro 2 ▪ 0577 941 862 ▪ Closed 10 Jan–10 Feb; mid Nov–Christmas; Mon Dec–Mar ▪ €€
Crisp tablecloths and excellent service are coupled with fascinating menus explaining the origins of each finely prepared dish (see p72).

2 Osteria delle Catene, San Gimignano
MAP D3 ▪ Via Mainardi 18 ▪ 0577 941 966 ▪ Closed Tue, Sun Dinner ▪ €
Dine in a softly lit brick-barrelled vault. Like any good osteria, this one serves great platters of mixed cheeses and cured meats, along with a good selection of wines.

3 La Mangiatoia, San Gimignano
MAP D3 ▪ Via Mainardi 5 ▪ 0577 941 094 ▪ Closed Sun ▪ €€
The more imaginative dishes at "The Trough" are excellent (though the standard fare seems perfunctorily prepared). Classical music adds to the lively atmosphere.

4 La Tana dei Brilli, Massa Marittima
MAP D4 ▪ Vicolo Ciambellano 4 ▪ 0566 901 274 ▪ Closed Wed ▪ €€
Italy's smallest Slow Food osteria is big on rustic charm. Dishes are rooted in the Maremma, using ingredients like chestnut flour and wild boar.

5 Trattoria del Sacco Fiorentino, Volterra
MAP D4 ▪ Via Giusto Turazza 13 ▪ 0588 88 537 ▪ Closed Wed ▪ €€
Enjoy superb wines and traditional seasonal specialities at this cosy central trattoria.

6 Taverna del Vecchio Borgo, Massa Marittima
MAP D4 ▪ Via Norma Parenti 12 ▪ 0566 903 950 ▪ Closed Mon, & Sun eve Oct–Mar ▪ €€
Suckling pigs roast on spits in the open fireplace. Try the tris di primi sampler of three first courses.

7 Del Duca, Volterra
MAP D4 ▪ Via di Castello 2 ▪ 0588 81 510 ▪ Closed Tue ▪ €€
Family-run restaurant specializing in historic Volterran cooking, overseen by convivial chef-owner Genuino.

The family-run Del Duca restaurant

8 Arnolfo, Colle di Val d'Elsa
MAP E3 ▪ Via XX Settembre 50–52a ▪ 0577 920 549 ▪ Closed Tue & Wed ▪ €€€
Refined cooking in a 15th-century palazzo. Sample the enormous wine cellar, which ranges from little-known locals to grand foreign wines.

9 Trattoria Albana, near Volterra
MAP D4 ▪ Mazzolla ▪ 0588 39 001 ▪ Closed Tue in winter & Tue lunch in summer ▪ €
This traditional trattoria appeared in the BBC's Trip to Italy series. Try the signature dish, ravioli with guinea fowl.

10 La Sosta di Pio VII, Barberino Val d'Elsa
MAP E3 ▪ "La Sosta del Papa" ▪ 055 807 5923 ▪ €
Simple dishes like pasta with rabbit ragù and tagliata (steak) with bitter radicchio let the ingredients sing.

See map on p114 ←

TOP10 Southern Tuscany

Montalcino
enoteca sign

If ever Bacchus blessed a landscape, it was the hilly terrain south of Siena. The dry clay soil is ideal for those Mediterranean plants: grapevines and olive trees. Two of Italy's mightiest red wines hail from these parts – Brunello di Montalcino and Vino Nobile di Montepulciano. And where even the vines can't take hold, grasslands thrive to provide rich grazing for sheep on the hills around Pienza, their milk producing the finest *pecorino* cheeses. Charming medieval hill towns, cypress-lined roads, isolated monasteries, Renaissance *palazzi*, Sienese School altarpieces and Etruscan tombs complete the picture.

Montepulciano

SOUTHERN TUSCANY

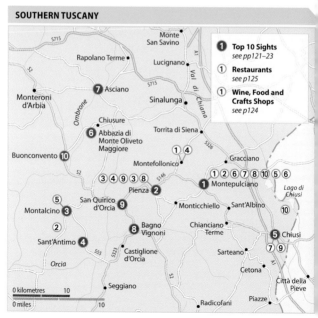

1 Top 10 Sights
see pp121–23

1 Restaurants
see p125

1 Wine, Food and Crafts Shops
see p124

1 Montepulciano

MAP F4 ▪ Tourist office: Piazza Don Minzoni 1 ▪ 0578 757 341 ▪ www.prolocomontepulciano.it

This hill town boasts buildings by major Renaissance architects and Tuscany's second greatest wine, Vino Nobile *(see p71)*. Via Gracciano nel Corso is lined with Renaissance *palazzi* by the likes of Vignola and Antonio da Sangallo the Elder, but also look out for Palazzo Bucelli (No. 73), its base embedded with Etruscan urns. The Piazza Grande is flanked by palaces by Sangallo, the town's Duomo and the Palazzo Comunale, which is Michelozzo's tribute to Florence's Palazzo Vecchio. Inside the Duomo are Michelozzo sculptures that once formed a single tomb, while the gilded altarpiece is Taddeo di Bartolo's Sienese Gothic masterpiece of 1401. Set on a patch of grass below the town walls is Sangallo's geometrically precise church of Tempio di San Biagio (1518–34), the best example of the High Renaissance trend towards Greek Cross churches *(see p61)*.

2 Pienza

MAP F4 ▪ Tourist office: Corso Rossellino 30 ▪ 0578 749 905 ▪ www.prolocopienza.it

In the 15th century, Pope Pius II hired Rossellino to revamp his home village. The resulting assemblage of buildings is now a UNESCO World Heritage Site, and includes a retro-Gothic town hall, a bishop's palace (now the Museo Diocesano with art by Pietro Lorenzetti, Vecchietta and Bartolo di Fredi), a papal palace with great hanging gardens and a Duomo

Wheels of cheese for sale, Pienza

(see p59). Corso Rossellino, the town's main street, is packed with wine and cheese shops.

3 Montalcino

MAP E4 ▪ Tourist office: Via Costa del Municipio 1 ▪ 0577 849 331 ▪ www.prolocomontalcino.com

The hometown of Brunello *(see p71)*, Tuscany's mightiest wine, is a small but proud burg, with an excellent wine shop in the ruined 14th-century *fortezza (see p124)*, a split-level main square and a lanky 1292 tower. The Museo Civico e Diocesano houses paintings by Simone Martini, Sano di Pietro and Vecchietta, and polychrome wood statues by Francesco di Valdambrino *(see p61)*.

4 Sant'Antimo

A French-style Romanesque abbey church standing in a beautiful countryside setting *(see p58)*.

The abbey of Sant'Antimo

Porsenna labyrinth tunnels, Chiusi

5 Chiusi
**MAP F5 ■ Tourist office:
Via Porsenna 79 ■ 0578 227 667
■ www.prolocochiusi.it/en**

Chiusi's fine Museo Archeologico Nazionale Etrusco contains *bucchero* (black Etruscan earthenware), a few 2nd-century-BC painted funerary urns, bronzes and Canopic jars. You can also buy tickets to visit the Etruscan tombs in the valley, including the Tombs of the Lion, the Pilgrim and the Monkey. The 12th-century Duomo is covered in trompe l'oeil frescoes (1887–94) that look like medieval mosaics. The adjacent Museo della Cattedrale preserves 15th-century illuminated scores from the Abbazia di Monte Oliveto Maggiore. Meet here for guided visits to the tunnels of the Etruscan Labirinto di Porsenna.

6 Abbazia di Monte Oliveto Maggiore
**MAP E4 ■ Monte Oliveto Maggiore
■ 0577 707 611 ■ 9:15am–noon & 3:15–5pm**

Nestled on a cypress-covered hilltop in the Crete Senesi landscape of eroded clay and limestone bluffs is a 1313 Benedictine monastery (see p75). Its cloister is frescoed with the *Life of St Benedict*, a masterpiece of High Renaissance narrative painting by Signorelli (the west wall's eight scenes; 1497–8) and Sodoma (the other 25 scenes; 1505–8). Sodoma inserted a self-portrait in the third scene, his pet badgers at his feet.

7 Asciano
**MAP E4 ■ Tourist office:
Via delle Fonti ■ 0577 718 811
■ www.prolocoasciano.it**

With 14th-century walls and a travertine Romanesque Collegiata, Asciano stands amid the photogenic Crete Senesi hills. Palazzo Corboli, decorated with 14th-century civic frescoes, holds the town's archae-ological and sacred art collections, with panels by Ambrogio Lorenzetti and others. The Cassioli Museum is the only museum in Siena province dedicated to art from the Sienese School of the 19th century.

8 Bagno Vignoni
MAP E5

Little more than houses around a vast, Medici-built portico and basin steaming with naturally carbonated, volcanically heated waters. Lorenzo the Magnificent and St Catherine both bathed here, but sadly the old basin is no longer in use. Today the thermal baths are run by the town-ship and offer a range of therapies.

The old basin at Bagno Vignoni

Collegiata carving, San Quirico

⑨ San Quirico d'Orcia
MAP E4 ▪ Tourist office: Via
Dante Alighieri 33 ▪ 0577 897 211

This is a friendly little farming town
that boasts amazing Romanesque
carvings on the Collegiata's trio of
12th-century portals: a variety of
fantastical creatures, stacked arches,
tiny telamons and thin columns
"knotted" in the centre and resting
on toothless lions. Inside is a sumptuous Sano di Pietro altarpiece.

⑩ Buonconvento
MAP E4 ▪ Tourist office:
Piazzale Garibaldi ▪ 0577 807 181
▪ www.terresiena.it

The tiny historic centre shelters a
good Museo d'Arte Sacra, holding
Sienese School works by Duccio,
Sano di Pietro and Matteo di
Giovanni, who also left a *Madonna
and Child* in the town's 14th-century
Santi Piero e Paolo church.

A DAY'S DRIVE

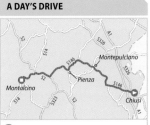

▶ **MORNING**

Start at 9am in **Chiusi**, at the
Museo Archeologico Nazionale
Etrusco. After learning about the
Etruscans, head across the piazza
to join a Labirinto di Porsenna
tour. They leave every 40 minutes,
so you might be able to squeeze
in a 10-minute tour of the Museo
della Cattedrale as well. Then
retrieve your car and take the
winding S146 to **Montepulciano**
(see p121). Park at the base of
town to stroll up Via Gracciano
nel Corso (its name changes
constantly), sampling wines along
the way. Stop for lunch at the
Liberty-style Caffè Poliziano (Via
Voltaio nel Corso 27–29), which
has served light meals with great
countryside views since 1858.

AFTERNOON

After lunch, continue up the main
street and pop inside the Gesù to
admire Andrea Pozzo's illusionary
painted "dome". Next head to the
Piazza Grande (more wine shops)
and then on to the Duomo. Then
drive on to **Pienza** *(see p121)* but
just before hitting the S146, stop
at Via dei Canneti at the edge of
Montepulciano to see the Tempio
di San Biagio (you can skip the
bare interior). Pienza is a quick
stop. After viewing the Duomo's
altarpieces *(see p59)* and the giant
cracks from the settling of the
cliff, tour Pope Pius II's Palazzo
Piccolomini. An alley next to the
palazzo leads to Via Gozzante, a
panoramic walkway out of town.
Drive on to **Montalcino** *(see p121)*.
In summer, head to the fortress
for sunset views from the ramparts; in winter, make your way to
the historic Caffè Fiaschetteria
Italiana in the main square.

See map on p120 ←

Wine, Food and Crafts Shops

Barrels of wine at Contucci

and candlesticks to fantastical chandeliers, all handmade the traditional way using hammer and anvil.

(5) Enoteca La Fortezza, Montalcino

MAP E4 ▪ La Fortezza ▪ Open Apr–Oct: 9am–8pm; Nov–Mar: 9am–6pm

The best selection of wine (and other goods) in town. Gorgeous setting in the airy remains of the medieval fortress.

(6) Aliseda, Montepulciano

MAP F4 ▪ Via dell'Opio nel Corso 8 ▪ Open 9:30am–8pm (summer closed Sun & Mon)

Unique (and pricey) gold jewellery, inspired by ancient museum pieces.

(1) Contucci, Montepulciano

MAP F4 ▪ Via del Teatro 1 ▪ Open 9:30am–7pm

This winemaker's labyrinthine cellars are inside a Renaissance palazzo on Piazza Grande. The range includes Vino Nobile DOCG wines and a sweet Vin Santo.

(2) Gattavecchi, Montepulciano

MAP F4 ▪ Via di Collazzi 74 ▪ Open 10:30am–7pm

Leading winery with grotto-like cellars. The shop sells their Vino Nobile wines as well as estate olive oil. There is a small tasting fee (see p70).

(3) La Bottega del Cacio, Pienza

MAP F4 ▪ Corso Rossellino 66 ▪ Open 9:30am–1pm & 3–7:30pm

Boutique with every kind of *pecorino* plus honey, pâtés, conserves and olive oils.

(4) Biagiotti & Figli, Pienza

MAP F4 ▪ Via I Maggio 1 ▪ Open 10:30am–1pm & 3–7pm

Cast and wrought iron of great beauty in everything from bedsteads

(7) Maledetti Toscani, Montepulciano

MAP F4 ▪ Via Voltaia nel Corso 40 ▪ Open 10am–7pm

A bit of everything handcrafted and Tuscan: leatherwork, wrought iron, copper pots and more.

(8) Bottega del Rame, Montepulciano

MAP F4 ▪ Via dell'Opio nel Corso 64 ▪ Open 9:30am–7:30pm

The Mazzetti family sells a range of beautiful hand-hammered copperware.

(9) Enoteca di Ghino, Pienza

MAP F4 ▪ Via del Leone 16 ▪ Open 9am–1pm & 2:30–7:30pm

One of Tuscany's best wine shops, with a good selection at almost every price.

Copper grapes, Bottega del Rame

(10) Legatoria Koiné, Montepulciano

MAP F4 ▪ Via Gracciano nel Corso 22 ▪ Open 9am–1pm & 4–8pm

Beautiful leather-bound books and albums, each individually crafted in their *bottega* using the best-quality vegetable-tanned leather.

Restaurants

PRICE CATEGORIES

For a three-course meal for one with half a bottle of wine (or equivalent meal), taxes and extra charges.

€ under €35   €€ €35–70   €€€ over €70

1 La Chiusa, Montefollonico

MAP F4 ■ Via della Madonnina 88 (near Montepulciano/Pienza) ■ 0577 848 044 ■ Closed Tue ■ €€€

Set in an 18th-century oil mill, La Chiusa serves creative Tuscan cooking using local, seasonal ingredients.

2 Ristorante del Poggio Antico, near Montalcino

MAP E4 ■ Loc 1 Poggi ■ 0577 849 200 ■ Closed Mon, Sun dinner (Nov–Mar) ■ €€

Refined restaurant in the converted stables of a top Brunello vineyard. Home-baked breads and innovative Tuscan cuisine. Booking advised.

3 Trattoria Latte di Luna, Pienza

MAP F4 ■ Via San Carlo 2–4 ■ 0578 748 606 ■ Closed Tue ■ €

Simple, soulful southern Tuscan cooking alfresco. Try the *pici* with garlicky tomatoes or the roast suckling pig.

4 La Botte Piena, near Montefollonico

MAP F4 ■ Piazza Cinughi 12, Torrita di Siena ■ 0577 669 481 ■ €€

Oak-beamed ceiling, stone and brick walls and food steeped in the traditions of the Sienese countryside.

5 Acquacheta, Montepulciano

MAP F4 ■ Via del Teatro 22 ■ 0578 717 086 ■ Closed Tue ■ €

This place is a shrine to the *bistecca*. Steaks are ordered by weight before being brought to the table for approval then cooked (briefly) on the flamegrill. Tasty sides include baked *pecorino* cheese with pear.

The elegant Ristorante La Grotta

6 Ristorante La Grotta, Montepulciano

MAP F4 ■ San Biagio 15 ■ 0578 757 479 ■ Closed Wed ■ €€

Top-class Tuscan cuisine is created in this beautiful Renaissance building with vaulted terracotta ceilings. The service is impeccable.

7 Ristorante Zaira, Chiusi

MAP F5 ■ Via Arunte 12 ■ 0578 20 260 ■ Closed Mon (winter) ■ €

Best eatery in a renowned culinary town. The speciality is *pasta del lucumone* ("Big King's pasta"), a baked casserole of ham and three cheeses.

8 Osteria Sette di Vino, Pienza

MAP F4 ■ Piazza di Spagna 1 ■ 0578 749 092 ■ €

Tiny *osteria* with great mixed platters of *pecorino* cheese and salamis and a secret-family-recipe salad dressing.

9 La Solita Zuppa, Chiusi

MAP F5 ■ Via Porsenna 21 ■ 0578 21 006 ■ Closed Tue; Jan & Feb ■ €€

A cosy spot offering southern Tuscan dishes such as *pici* with duck sauce.

10 La Fattoria, Lago di Chiusi

MAP F4 ■ Via Lago di Chiusi (5km east of Chiusi) ■ 0578 21 407 ■ €

Converted farmhouse/inn by Chiusi's lake, which provides the fresh catch of the day. The prosciutto is hand-carved, the pasta home-made and the lake view tranquil.

See map on p120 ←

🔟 The Southern Coast and Maremma

This is Tuscany's undiscovered corner, a largely flat area with a few low hills capped by crumbling ancient hill towns such as Pitigliano and Sorano. Its overgrown valleys hide Etruscan tombs, altars and sunken roads *(see p128)*. This was the heart of Etruria, a fertile breadbasket and home to important Etruscan cities. But the conquering Romans were not as adept at maintaining large-scale drainage and irrigation systems, and this agricultural paradise quickly reverted to malarial swampland. The population dwindled, the ancient cities crumbled and most Tuscan powers left the Maremma alone. It was not until 1828 that Grand Duke Leopold I started draining the land again. Today, it is Tuscany's least disturbed repository of Etruscan heritage, while also offering beaches, Tuscany's best natural park and the Tyrrhenian islands.

A view of Pitigliano

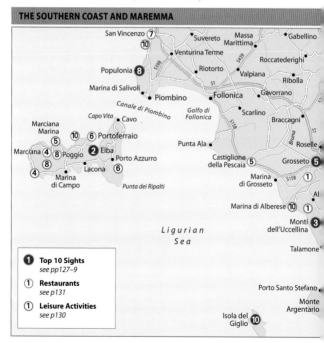

THE SOUTHERN COAST AND MAREMMA

1 Top 10 Sights
see pp127–9

1 Restaurants
see p131

1 Leisure Activities
see p130

1 Pitigliano

MAP F6 ▪ Tourist office: Piazza Garibaldi 51 ▪ 0564 617 111 ▪ Jewish quarter tours on Wed, Fri, Sun ▪ www.turismoinmaremma.it

Etruscan Pitigliano seems to grow right out of its rocky terrain. This hill town's greatest sight is its medieval self, though the Palazzo Orsini castle (a 13th-century structure, enlarged by Giuliano da Sangallo) houses – apart from its own rooms – a few modest museums of local Etruscan finds, including the Museo Civico Archeologico. The synagogue offers tours of Pitigliano's tiny, labyrinthine Jewish ghetto, which all but vanished after Nazi deportations (see p61).

2 Elba

MAP C5 ▪ Tourist office: Calata Italia 43, Portoferraio ▪ 0565 914 671 ▪ www.visitelba.info

This modestly scaled resort island, with its great beaches, derives its name from Aethalia, the Greek word

Cavoli beach on the island of Elba

for the sparks of its busy iron forges. Portoferraio, where ferries arrive from Piombino, has three forts, Napoleon's Villa dei Mulini (his Villa San Martino south of town is more interesting, however), and a small archaeological museum. Porto Azzuro was the island's Spanish capital and is today a bustling resort that retains something of the old fishing town. Hilltop Capoliveri has the best nightlife and evocative medieval alleyways. Marciana is a good hill-town base for exploring the island's western half (see p67).

3 Monti dell'Uccellina

MAP E6 ▪ Park entrance at Albarese ▪ 0564 407 098 ▪ 7am–dusk (9am–dusk Oct–14 Jun) ▪ Adm ▪ www.parco-maremma.it

The greatest protected parkland in Tuscany, coastal Monti dell'Uccellina ("Mountains of the Little Bird") is a large area of pine forests teeming with boar, roe deer and porcupines, bird-filled marshland to the north and tracts of pristine beach. A pack of wild horses and roaming long-horned white Maremma cattle are looked after by Butteri cowboys. Buses from Albarese take you to the centre of the park.

4 Monte Argentario

MAP E6 ▪ Tourist office: Corso Umberto 55, Porto Santo Stefano ▪ 0564 814 208 ▪ www.turismoinmaremma.it

This quietly chic and beautiful peninsula is really an almost-circular island, connected to the Tuscan mainland by causeways (see p67).

5 Grosseto

MAP E5 ■ Tourist office: Via Monterosa 206 ■ 0564 462 611 ■ www.turismoinmaremma.it

Grubby Grosseto lacks real charm, but Museo Civico Archeologico e d'Arte della Maremma showcases superb Etruscan artifacts. Many of the more portable finds from the Maremma are housed here, along with works of art from city churches, including Guido da Siena's 13th-century *Last Judgement* and a Sassetta *Madonna of the Cherries*. The 13th-century church of San Francesco has fresco fragments and a high altar *Crucifix* (1285) attributed to Duccio.

The Duomo of Sovana

6 Sovana

MAP F6

This modest hamlet was once an Etruscan city, Roman *municipium*, and birthplace of 11th-century Aldobrandeschi Pope Gregory VII, who reigned for 12 years. On the main square are a medieval Palazzo Pretorio and the church of Santa Maria, which contains 15th-century frescoes and a rare 9th-century altar canopy. Built between the 8th and 13th centuries, the Duomo on the edge of town preserves carvings from the Dark Ages. The surrounding hills and valley are dotted with signposted Etruscan tombs, altars and *vie cave*; the best is the Tomba Ildebranda *(see p68)*.

7 Saturnia

MAP E6

Visitors come to Saturnia not for the little town and its 15th-century

THE VIE CAVE

No one is sure why the Etruscans dug these "sunken roads", narrow canyons up to 20 m (65 ft) deep into the rocky ground of the Maremma. Many extend for kilometres between settlements. They may have been defensive, religious (some led to tombs or altars), for herding or perhaps some mixture of all these possibilities.

Sienese castle but to take the waters. The valley's warm, mineral-rich waters feed a four-star spa (which is elegant, but smells of rotten eggs), a hotel and the lovely Cascate del Gorello, which gushes down a hillside, running into small pools and waterfalls *(see p66)*.

8 Populonia

MAP C5 ■ Baratti ■ 0565 29 002 ■ Necropolis: open Mar–May, Oct: 10am–6pm Tue–Sun; Jul & Aug: 9:30am–7:30pm daily; Jun & Sep: 10am–7pm Tue–Sun; Nov–Feb: 10am–4pm Sat & Sun ■ Adm ■ www.parchivaldicornia.it

Baratti Bay's Iron Age role as port for Elba's mines helped preserve Populonia's Etruscan necropolis – under a slag heap. Half a dozen of the tombs are visitable, several almost intact. Museo Gasparri holds many of the items excavated here.

Isola del Giglio

The ancient hill town of Sorano

9 Sorano
MAP F5 ■ Tourist office: Piazza Busati ■ 0564 633 099
■ www.comune.sorano.gr.it

Sorano is an ancient Etruscan hill town literally slipping off its rocky outcrop. The restored 11th-century Aldobrandeschi fortress (expanded by the Orsini in 1552) is now part medieval museum, part small hotel (see p143). The town's 18th-century Massa Leopoldino fortress is also open to visitors.

10 Isola del Giglio
MAP D6 ■ Tourist office: Via Provinciale 9 ■ 0564 809 400
■ www.isoladelgiglio.it

This hilly isle off l'Argentario (ferries from Porto Santo Stefano) has the medieval hamlet of Castello above the docks, a beach at the port and an even better low-key resort and beach on the bay at Campese. Ansonico, the local wine, is known mainly to the habitués who crowd here on summer weekends.

THE BEST OF THE MAREMMA IN A DAY

▶ MORNING

Begin your day in **Saturnia**. Skip the spa and head straight to the **Cascate del Gorello** open-air hot springs south of town, where you can wallow in the wonderful natural whirlpools for free.

After your mineral soak, drive east towards Sovana. Look for roadside signs indicating Etruscan ruins (tomba, ipogeo) and semi-subterranean paths cut through the soft volcanic tufa rock (vie cave). Explore as many as you can – especially the spectacular **Tomba Ildebranda** – before heading into **Sovana** for lunch. Pop into Santa Maria church and the Duomo, which preserves good carvings, some predating the Romanesque era.

AFTERNOON

Continue east to **Sorano** to visit the Fortezza degli Orsini (it reopens for the afternoon at 3pm), an 11th-century fort which also hosts a museum dedicated to the medieval and Renaissance periods. Afterwards take some time to poke around the abandoned cliffside neighbourhood of Via delle Rovine.

End your day in the most dramatic of the Maremma's hill towns, **Pitigliano** (see p127). Make sure you arrive by 5pm in order to enter the town's ultramodern archaeological museum, set within a fortified palazzo. The town's labyrinthine Jewish ghetto and museum is open a little later. Then head to the panoramic balcony just beyond the eastern gate to watch the evening lights come on over a town that seems to grow from bare rock.

See map on pp126–7

Leisure Activities

Parco Naturale della Maremma

1 Parco Naturale della Maremma and Monti dell'Uccellina Trails

MAP E5 ▪ Trails 3 & 4 occasionally closed Jun–Sep ▪ Adm

"Strada degli Olivi" beelines for the beach. Trail 1 (7.2 km/4.5 miles) explores San Rabano abbey's ruins. Trail 2 (6 km/4 miles) goes past medieval towers to the rocky shore. Trail 3 (9.6 km/6 miles) meanders amid prehistoric caves. Trail 4 (12 km/7.5 miles) wanders everywhere.

2 Exploring Etruscan Tombs

MAP F6 ▪ www.leviecave.it

Get a map in Sovana or at Sorano's fortress to explore the tombs and *vie cave* hidden in the countryside.

3 Saturnia's Hot Springs
MAP E6

Relaxing hot springs *(see p66)*.

4 Elba's Beaches
MAP C5

Boats can whisk you to secluded beaches on the northeast shore. The western coast has rocky shoals good for snorkelling and, around Fetovaia, sandy beaches on tiny inlets.

5 Scuba and Snorkelling on Elba

MAP C5 ▪ Elba Diving Centre, Viale Aldo Moro 42, Marciana Marina ▪ 339 733 8902 ▪ www.elbadiving.it

Basic lessons, full courses, rentals and guided day and night dives.

6 Sailing and Windsurfing on Elba

MAP C5 ▪ Aloha Center, Spiaggia di Narengo, Capoliveri ▪ 347 496 9219 or 339 653 6447 ▪ www.alohacenter.it

Rent sailboards, catamarans and Zodiacs, or take windsurfing and sailing courses.

7 Horse Riding on the Coast

MAP E6 ▪ Il Barbazzale di Amalfitano, Via Aurelia 146, Orbetello Scalo ▪ 3481 457 737 ▪ www.maneggioilbarbazzale.com

Guided rides set off from an Orbetello lagoon base. Moonlit rides take place from June to September.

8 Hiking on Elba
MAP C5

Tourist office brochures lay out 12 hikes from 90 minutes to all day. The most rewarding is up (or down – you may ride the cable car one way) the Monte Capenne, past Sanctuario di San Cerbone church.

9 Scuba around Monte Argentario

MAP E6 ▪ Pelagos Diving Centre, Lungomare A Doria 11–13, Porto Ercole ▪ 0564 834 200 ▪ www.pelagosdc.com

Equipment rentals, lessons, guided dives and snorkelling around the islands of Giglio and Giannutri and Monte Argentario.

10 Etruscan Coast Beaches
MAP C3

The "Etruscan Coast" to the south of Livorno includes pine-shaded, sandy, semi-secluded Marina di Albarese and the resort of San Vincenzo.

Restaurants

1 ## Ristorante Gli Attortellati, Grosseto

MAP E5 ■ Strada Provinciale della Trappola 39 ■ 0564 400 059 ■ Closed Sun dinner, Mon, Tue–Fri lunch ■ €

Advance booking is essential at this award-winning *agriturismo* serving delicious Maremmana dishes.

2 ## Da Caino, Montemerano

MAP E6 ■ Via Chiesa 4 ■ 0564 602 817 ■ Closed Wed ■ €€€

A rustic but elegant room in the Maremma. The cooking is inspired by regional recipes and seasonal ingredients. Bread and pasta are homemade, and the wine list is vast.

3 ## Il Tufo Allegro, Pitigliano

MAP F6 ■ Vicolo della Constituzione 5 ■ 0564 616 192 ■ Closed Tue, Wed lunch (except Aug) ■ €

A young-spirited place, where Domenico adds creative touches to local ingredients and Valeria suggests accompanying wines.

4 ## Osteria del Noce, Elba

MAP C5 ■ Via della Madonna 14, Marciana ■ 0565 901 284 ■ €€

The softly lit rustic dining room has a pergola-shaded terrace with sea views. The owners' native Liguria is evident in the cooking.

5 ## Osteria nel Buco, Castiglione della Pescaia

MAP D5 ■ Via del Recinto 11 ■ 0564 934 460 ■ Closed Mon (except mid-Jun–mid-Sep) ■ €

Small cellar *osteria* in this fishing village/resort. The Maremmana food is excellent, balancing meat and seafood, and the gregarious owner carries a good tune.

6 ## Osteria Libertaria, Elba

MAP C5 ■ Calata Matteotti 12, Portoferraio ■ 0565 914 978 ■ €€

Portside dining in a scenic spot. Simple grilled fish or a *fritto misto* (catch-dependent mixed fry) are good choices, but also try traditional dishes like *riso nero* (rice blackened with squid ink).

7 ## La Barcaccina, San Vincenzo

MAP C4 ■ Via Tridentina 1 ■ 0565 701 911 ■ Closed Nov–Mar, also Wed Apr, May, Sep & Oct ■ €€

Kick off your shoes for some serious seafood cooking right on the sand.

8 ## Publius, Elba

MAP C5 ■ Piazza Castagneto 11, Poggio, Marciana ■ 0565 99 208 ■ Closed Mon Oct–May & Mon lunch Jun–Sep ■ €€

Family-run for four decades, this refined restaurant has a jaw-dropping perch in the Elban hills.

9 ## La Taverna Etrusca, Sovana

MAP F6 ■ Piazza del Pretorio 16 ■ 0564 614 113 ■ €

Good Tuscan cuisine in a room framed by beamed ceilings and stone archways dating to the 1200s.

10 ## Emanuel, Elba

MAP C5 ■ Loc Enfola, near Portoferraio ■ 0565 939 003 ■ Closed Oct–May ■ €€

An unassuming beachfront shack serving Elba's best seafood and excellent desserts. The tiny courtyard at the back leads onto the pebble beach.

The pleasant courtyard at Emanuel

See map on pp126–7

Streetsmart

A pair of Vespa scooters on a street
in Arezzo, Eastern Tuscany

Getting To and Around Florence and Tuscany

Arriving by Air

Almost all transatlantic and intercontinental flights to Italy land in **Rome Fiumicino** or **Milan Malpensa**, from where you can get connecting flights to Pisa or to Florence. Rome and Milan both have fast train links to Florence, or you can rent a car and drive to Tuscany.

Pisa Galileo Galilei, the biggest international airport in Tuscany, has multiple connections to the UK and to most European countries. A **Terravision** coach service links the airport to Florence in 70 minutes. The PisaMover transit service (operated by Trenitalia) takes only 5 or 6 minutes from the airport to Pisa Centrale station, from where it is about an hour by train to Florence, half an hour to Lucca or 2 hours to Siena.

Florence Peretola (Amerigo Vespucci) airport is smaller and offers direct flights only to major European capitals and business cities. City-centre transfers are operated by **Volainbus**, a 20-minute shuttle that connects every half an hour to the Autostazione, Florence's main bus station. Tickets are sold in the airport arrivals hall. Taxis wait outside and charge a fixed price to central Florence.

Arriving by Rail

Florence's Santa Maria Novella Station is the rail gateway to Tuscany, with high-speed connections north to Venice and Milan, and south to Rome and Naples, operated by **Trenitalia** and private company **Italo**. High-speed trains need reservations with allocated seating. For the cheapest prices, book between 90 and 120 days in advance. Domestic high-speed rail travel is ticketless: all you need to show the conductor is your booking code on paper or smartphone.

Loco2 is a useful site for booking European rail travel. You can take the train from London to Florence via a Eurostar to Paris, then TGV to Milan, and Italy's high-speed line for the final leg to Tuscany. From Paris to Italy, you can also use **Thello**. International connections from France, Germany, Switzerland and Austria are routed to Tuscany via either Milan or Verona.

Florence is connected by train to Arezzo, Pistoia, Prato, Montecatini, Lucca, Viareggio, Empoli, Livorno and Pisa. Each station posts departures on a yellow poster, arrivals on white and updates on digital screens. Before boarding a local train, stamp your ticket at the platform's yellow box or risk a fine. In Florence left luggage is next to track 16.

Arriving by Coach

Long-distance coaches from Italy and farther afield in Europe are operated by **Eurolines**. They can be slower and are no cheaper than trains, but they do serve towns that are inaccessible by rail. Especially useful is the Florence–Siena *rapida* fast service operated by **Toscana Mobilità**, which is quicker and more regular than the rail connection.

Arriving by Car

Italy's main highway, the A1 *autostrada*, comes from Milan via Bologna to Florence, then goes on to Rome and Naples. The A12 skirts the west coast from Genoa past Pisa, ending near Livorno, where it merges with state road S1 heading south through the Maremma. The A11 links Viareggio to Florence via Lucca and Pistoia.

The only efficient way to explore Tuscany's back roads, hill towns and vineyards is by car. Local outfits are rarely cheaper than the web, so it is wise to prebook from home. Try rental aggregator sites such as **Auto Europe**. Carry a good map, because signage away from the *autostrada* is erratic. Road signs (blue for a state road, green for an *autostrada*) usually indicate a destination. Route numbers are rarely mentioned.

Often ignored, speed limits are 30–50 kmph (20–30 mph) in town, 80–110 kmph (50–70 mph) on two-lane roads, and 130 kmph (80 mph) on the *autostrada*. Left lanes are for passing (in theory).

Tuscany's only toll roads are the A1, A11, and A12. Many filling stations close on Sundays, though often there are automated dispensers that take banknotes and sometimes credit cards.

Few urban hotels have their own parking, though many have deals with nearby garages. Legal street parking is always marked: yellow-lined spaces are reserved for officials such as the *carabinieri*, white spaces are for residents and blue spaces are available for an hourly fee, to be prepaid at a nearby machine. Display the ticket on your dashboard.

Driving in Florence's historic core is prohibited for anyone without a ZTL permit, but visitors are allowed to call at their hotel to deposit bags. You can then drive your car to one of several garages operated in the city by **Firenze Parcheggi**.

Florence also has three car-sharing companies, **Share'ngo**, **car2go** and **Enjoy**. These are a good alternative for those who only need a car for a few hours or so.

Taxi

Taxis wait at airports and stations, and any hotel or restaurant will call you a cab. Taxis can be ordered online or by phone from **4242** or **4390** in Florence and **RadioTaxi Pisa** in Pisa. Rates go up for trips outside the city centre, on Sundays, with luggage and after 8pm. Because of a tortuous one-way system, Florence taxis can be expensive for seemingly short trips.

City Bus and Tram

Florence city buses are operated by **ATAF**. Buy tickets at tobacconists', bars, newsstands or (at a premium) on the bus.

Stamp your ticket on the bus (*autobus*) when you board. Tickets last for 90 minutes, during which you can transfer bus as often as you like. Florence's pedestrianized core is crossed by four minibus (*bussini*) lines, C1, C2, C3 and D. Buses run from 7am to 9pm. The ATAF website has route maps. The city's original **tram** line, T1, runs from 5am to midnight from the centre to the suburb of Scandicci. Two further tram lines opened in early 2018.

Bicycle and Foot

No historic town centre in Tuscany takes more than 30 minutes to cross on foot. Many streets are cobblestoned, however, so wear comfortable shoes. Florence is increasingly bike-friendly, with some pretty riverside cycle lanes. Cyclists can rent bikes by the hour, day or week at **Florence by Bike**.

DIRECTORY

ARRIVING BY AIR

Florence Peretola
w aeroporto.firenze.it

Milan Malpensa
w milanomalpensa-airport.com

Pisa Galileo Galilei
w pisa-airport.com

Rome Fiumicino
w adr.it

Terravision
w terravision.eu

Volainbus
w fsbusitalia.it

ARRIVING BY RAIL

Italo
w italotreno.it

Loco2
w loco2.com

Thello
w thello.com

Trenitalia
w trenitalia.com

ARRIVING BY COACH

Eurolines
w eurolines.it

Toscana Mobilità
w tiemmespa.it

ARRIVING BY CAR

Auto Europe
w autoeurope.com

car2go
w car2go.com

Enjoy
w enjoy.eni.com

Firenze Parcheggi
w firenzeparcheggi.it

Share'ngo
w site.sharengo.it

TAXI

4242
w 4242.it

4390
w 4390.it

RadioTaxi Pisa
w cotapi.it/en

CITY BUS AND TRAM

ATAF
w ataf.net

Tram
w gestramvia.com

BICYCLE AND FOOT

Florence by Bike
w florencebybike.it

Practical Information

Passports and Visas

Visitors from outside the European Economic Area (EEA), European Union (EU) and Switzerland need a valid passport to enter Italy. EEA, EU and Swiss nationals can use identity cards instead. Those from Canada, the US, Australia and New Zealand can stay for up to 90 days without a visa as long as their passport is valid for 6 months beyond the date of entry. Most other non-EU nationals need a valid passport and visa, and should consult the **Ministero degli Affari Esteri** website or their Italian embassy. Schengen visas are valid for Italy.

Customs and Immigration

For EU citizens there are no limits or duties on most goods carried in or out of Italy as long as they are for personal use only. Exceptions include firearms and weapons, certain types of food and plants, endangered species, pets, drugs and over €10,000 in cash.

For non-EU travellers, limits on personal items are 200 cigarettes or 250g (9 oz) of tobacco, one litre of spirits or four litres of wine, and goods with a value up to €430 (apart from personal luggage). Prescription medicines should be in original containers, and you should carry the prescription. Travellers cannot bring in meat or milk from outside Europe, and must declare any animal products, fruit,

vegetables or plants on arrival. Non-EU residents can also claim back sales tax on purchases over €155 *(see p140)*.

Travel Safety Advice

Visitors can get up-to-date travel safety information from the **Department of Foreign Affairs and Trade** in Australia, the **Foreign and Commonwealth Office** in the UK and the **State Department** in the US.

Travel Insurance

It is advisable to take out insurance against illness, accidents, theft or loss and travel cancellations, curtailment or delays. Emergency treatment or *pronto soccorso* is given free of charge at public hospitals, but specialist and follow-up treatment or repatriation are costly. EU residents will receive medical care under the public healthcare system if they have with them a valid European Health Insurance Card (EHIC). Prescriptions may have to be paid for upfront. Italy also has reciprocal agreements with Australian Medicare, but all other nationals should make sure they have insurance.

Emergency Services

The ambulance, police and fire brigade can be reached on the Europe-wide **emergency** number 112. The operators speak English. There are also dedicated lines for the **ambulance** and **fire brigade** as well as for

car breakdown assistance (this is a paid towing service).

Health

Italian hospitals *(ospedali)* are semi-privatized and efficient. An emergency room is *pronto soccorso*. For uncomplicated treatment, they'll usually check you over and write a prescription if needed, with no other paperwork involved. The most central hospital in Florence is **Ospedale Santa Maria Nuova**.

Italian pharmacies *(farmacie)* are signalled by a green cross and are usually well equipped in treating minor ailments. If a pharmacy is closed there will be a notice on display giving the location of the nearest open pharmacy. The central **Farmacia Comunale di Santa Maria Novella** in Florence is open 24/7.

Italian water is safe to drink except from train taps and any source indicated *"acqua non potabile"*. No vaccinations are required for visitors to Italy.

Personal Security

There are two police forces, the Carabinieri, the military branch, and the **Polizia di Stato**, the civil branch. The **Questura di Firenze** (*polizia* headquarters) is centrally located. You must report crimes if you wish to make an insurance claim.

Italy is generally safe and violent crime is rare, though women might receive unwelcome propositions. All travellers should avoid deserted back streets and empty parks at night. Begging is tolerated, and is visible around major tourist attractions. Pickpockets operate on buses, around stations and in other busy spots. Any property found on a bus or train in Florence is sent to the **Ufficio Oggetti Smarriti**.

Many Italians drive aggressively, so be careful behind the wheel, especially on the *autostrada*.

Disabled Travellers

Disabled travellers are admitted free to most museums and sights, and many places have adaptations for blind visitors, including the Uffizi's tactile re-creation of the *Birth of Venus (see p12)*.

Hotels generally have at least one accessible room, although many historic properties cannot accommodate guests with limited mobility.

All **ATAF buses** *(see p135)* are wheelchair-adapted. The Florence **tram** *(see p135)* has electric ramps for wheelchairs, and platforms have navigation aids for blind passengers. To book an adapted taxi, call **4242** or **4390** *(see p135)* at least 24 hours ahead of time.

Trips and Tours

Aggregators like **Viator** sell a range of city walks in Tuscany's main towns. **Context** has a matchless range of specialist walks in Florence, Pisa, Lucca, Siena and rural Tuscany. **I Just Drive** runs small-group private tours of Chianti with a driver.

Tuscany offers terrain both tough enough for die-hard pedallers and easy enough for dabblers. **I Bike Italy** runs several itineraries, including Florence day tours and multiday trips around Chianti. **Florence by Bike** *(see p135)* has short city photography rides plus Chianti trips, or will just rent you a bike.

For horse-riding trips in the Maremma or Chianti, try **Equitours** or **Il Paretaio**.

Learn to make *ribollita* soup, stuffed pastas and the perfect *bistecca* in Tuscany. Chianti's top school was founded by Lorenza de' Medici and is taught in English at **Badia a Coltibuono** abbey *(see p39)*, currently by chef Benedetta Vitali. In central Florence, courses last from a few hours to several weeks at the **Giglio Cooking School** and the **Cucina Lorenzo de' Medici**.

DIRECTORY

PASSPORTS AND VISAS

Ministero degli Affari Esteri
w vistoperitalia.esteri.it

CONSULATES

USA (Florence)
MAP J3 ■ Lungarno Vespucci 38
w it.usembassy.gov/ambasciata-e-consolati/firenze

TRAVEL SAFETY ADVICE

Australia
Department of Foreign Affairs and Trade
w smartraveller.gov.au

United Kingdom
Foreign and Commonwealth Office
w gov.uk/foreign-travel-advice

United States
US Department of State
w travel.state.gov

EMERGENCY SERVICES

Ambulance
📞 118

Car Breakdowns
📞 116

Emergency, Carabinieri
📞 112

Fire Brigade
📞 115

HEALTH

Farmacia Comunale di Santa Maria Novella
MAP L1 ■ Piazza della Stazione 1
📞 055 289 435/216 761

Ospedale Santa Maria Nuova
MAP P3 ■ Piazza S Maria Nuova 1
w asf.toscana.it

PERSONAL SECURITY

Polizia di Stato
📞 113
w poliziadistato.it

Questura di Firenze
Via Zara 2
📞 055 49 771

Ufficio Oggetti Smarriti
Via Veracini 5
📞 055 334 802

TRIPS AND TOURS

Badia a Coltibuono
w en.coltibuono.com

Context
w contexttravel.com

Cucina Lorenzo de' Medici
w cucinaldm.com

Equitours
w equitours.com

Giglio Cooking School
w gigliocooking.com

I Bike Italy
w ibikeitaly.com

I Just Drive
w ijustdrive.us

Il Paretaio
w ilparetaio.it

Viator
w viator.com

Currency and Banking

Italy is one of the 19 European countries using the euro (€), which is divided into 100 cents. Paper notes are in denominations of €5, €10, €20, €50, €100, €200 and €500. Coins are €2, €1, 50c, 20c, 10c, 5c, 2c and 1c. Small establishments will baulk at changing anything bigger than a €50 (cafés and newsstands prefer a €20 or smaller).

The easiest way to get local currency is from an ATM (bancomat) using a debit card. The exchange rate is also usually better this way. Inform your bank of your travel plans before departure to avoid having your card blocked for fraud protection.

Exchange money at a bank for the best rates – those at shops and hotels are rarely good. Cambio exchange booths are only good for emergencies out of banking hours. Prepaid currency cards (cash passports) are a more secure way of carrying money. They can be loaded with euros, fixing exchange rates before you leave, and used like a debit card.

Most restaurants, shops and hotels in cities and towns will accept Visa and MasterCard. American Express is accepted in many upscale places. Diners Club is usually only for luxury places (and even then, not always).

Internet and Telephone

Almost every hotel now provides Wi-Fi, usually free, and there are free Wi-Fi hotspots in squares and public buildings in many cities. Florence's **Firenze Card** includes three days of Wi-Fi and the **Mercato Centrale** has free Wi-Fi upstairs. In smaller towns, you may find an internet point in a store or bar.

TIM, Vodafone, 3 and Wind sell basic phones for under €30. They can be topped up by buying a *ricarica* (refill) at *tabacchi*, newsstands and supermarkets. If you have an unlocked GSM phone, you can buy a *ricaricabile* (pay-as-you-go or prepaid) local SIM and slot it into your handset – much cheaper than roaming.

Postal Services

Italy's post service, **Poste Italiane**, while improving, can be slow. Florence's **Central Post Office** is a 4-minute walk south of the Duomo. However, you needn't visit a post office (ufficio postale) to send a letter; tobacconists or newsagents can sell the right stamps (francobolli). Drop your letters in the postbox slot (usually red) that is labelled "per tutte le altre destinazioni", not "per la città".

Newspapers and Television

Train stations and central newsstands are best for finding English-language magazines and newspapers, including USA Today, The Times (London) and the International New York Times. Tuscany's main daily newspapers are **La Nazione** (Florence and around) and **Il Tirreno** (by the coast). Florence's main listings magazine, **Firenze Spettacolo**, is sold at newsstands and has an English-language section. **The Florentine** is a website and monthly magazine in English covering news, events and culture in and around Florence. The **Life in Italy** website covers Italian life and news in English. To read, watch or listen to British and world news online go to the BBC website. Most hotels have satellite or cable TV with CNN and BBC News.

Opening Hours

Shops, businesses and churches traditionally open at 8 or 9am, shut for *riposo* from 12:30 or 1pm to 3pm, then reopen until 6 to 8pm. In larger cities, however, the *riposo* is disappearing in favour of *orario continuato* (straight through) for chain stores and other shops. Post office hours are usually 8:20am–7pm weekdays, 8:20am–12:30pm on Saturdays. Standard banking hours are usually 8:30am to 1 or 1:30pm and from 3 until 4:15pm. Museum opening times vary, but 9am to 5pm is common. A few still close during the *riposo*, especially outside big cities.

Italian national holidays are: New Year's Day, Epiphany (6 Jan), Easter Sunday and Monday, Liberation Day (25 Apr), Workers' Day (1 May), Republic Day (2 Jun), *Ferragosto* (15 Aug), All Saints' Day (1 Nov), Immaculate Conception (8 Nov), Christmas Day (25 Dec) and St Stephen's Day (26 Dec). Several services, particularly hose aimed at locals, close on these days. Towns also shut down for the feast day of their saint.

Time Difference

Italy operates on Central European Time (CET), which is 1 hour ahead of Greenwich Mean Time and 6 hours ahead of US Eastern Standard Time. The clock moves forward 1 hour during daylight saving time from the last Sunday in March until the last Sunday in October.

Electrical Appliances

Italian electricity runs on 220V/50Hz. To use a 110V device, you will need a converter. To plug in, you will need an adaptor that fits continental Europe's standard two round pins.

Driving Licences

To rent a car you usually need to be over 20 and to have held a full driving licence for at least one year. It is recommended

that all non-EU visitors carry an International Driving Permit (IDP). When you pick up the vehicle, you'll need your licence, passport and a credit card with which to give a security deposit.

Weather

Tuscany has a generally warm climate, although the July and August heat can be brutal, especially in landlocked Florence. Up in the hills, it often snows in midwinter, and cold winds roar down from the Apennine mountains. Spring's middle ground keeps hotels booked, but autumn, when grapes (September) and olives (October) are harvested and boar and truffles hunted, is the true Tuscan time of year.

It is wise to bring one nice outfit, although few restaurants require jacket and tie. Many churches do not allow you to enter with bare shoulders or knees; a scarf or light shawl draped around the waist or shoulders gets you through the door.

Visitor Information

ENIT (Ente Nazionale Italiano per il Turismo) is the state tourism board, and provides basic information. Official tourist information offices are better for detailed information and inspiration. **Florence Tourism** has five offices in the city (including at the airport and main train station), all listed on their website. The **Tuscany Regional Tourism** portal is also useful. Local informazioni turistiche offices (often signed "Pro Loco") are good for free maps, opening hours and hotel directories, and usually respond to email requests for specific assistance. Many will also book a hotel or B&B if you arrive without a room (a risky strategy in high season).

If you can read Italian (or use Google Translate), the best Florence blog for restaurant news and events is **Io Amo Firenze**. Mary McCarthy's Stones of Florence is sublime and forthright on architecture.

DIRECTORY

INTERNET AND TELEPHONE

Firenze Card
w firenzecard.it

Mercato Centrale
MAP M2 ▪ Piazza del Mercato Centrale
w mercatocentrale.it

POSTAL SERVICES

Central Post Office
MAP M4 ▪ Via Pellicceria 3
📞 055 273 6481

Poste Italiane
w poste.it

NEWSPAPERS AND TELEVISION

Firenze Spettacolo
w firenzespettacolo.it

The Florentine
w theflorentine.net

Life in Italy
w lifeinitaly.com

La Nazione
w lanazione.it

Il Tirreno
w iltirreno.gelocal.it

VISITOR INFORMATION

ENIT
w enit.it

Florence Tourism
Information Office
MAP N2 ▪ Via Cavour 1r
Mon–Fri 9am–6pm (to 2pm Sat)
📞 055 290832
w firenzeturismo.it/en/

Io Amo Firenze
w ioamofirenze.it

Tuscany Regional Tourism
w turismo.intoscana.it

Shopping

Florentines are masters of the craft of marbled paper, creating intricate designs by swirling oil-based inks on the surface of a tray of water and then dipping the paper in it. **Il Papiro** sells affordable paper products across Italy, including in Siena (see p98), Florence, Pisa and Cortona.

Tuscany has a great reputation for leather – jackets, bags, wallets, shoes and belts can be found all over the region. **Madova** is the best choice for gloves. Upscale stationery shops such as **Legatoria Koiné** (see p124) handbind journals with leather. There is something for all budgets in Florence, from stalls in **San Lorenzo Market** (see p85) to boutiques in Via Tornabuoni and the Santa Croce **Scuola del Cuoio** leather school (see p85).

Florence is the home of **Gucci**, **Ferragamo** and **Pucci** (see p85). Gucci and **Prada** also have outlet stores in Tuscany (see p92 and p106), although in general high fashion is rarely cheaper than in other countries.

Tuscan wine, especially from Chianti, Montalcino or Montepulciano (see pp70–71), makes a good souvenir, although shipping is expensive.

Tuscany's ceramics tradition encompasses everything from Richard-Ginori porcelain and classy **Rampini** designs (see p92) to the traditional rustic patterns of Cortona, Siena and Montepulciano.

Some vintage shops can be found near Florence's Piazza dei Ciompi. Haggling is expected in markets, much less so in shops.

Italy's value added tax (IVA), currently 22 per cent, is a sales tax incorporated into every price tag. If you live outside the EU and spend more than €155 in one shop, you can get the tax refunded (see p136). Ask the store to help you fill out the forms, then take these with receipts to the customs office at your point of departure. Your refund may take a month or two to come through.

Dining

Traditionally, a *ristorante* is the most formal and expensive kind of eatery; a trattoria a family-run, moderately-priced joint; an *osteria* anything from a trattoria to a bar serving a few hot dishes; and a *tavola calda* is a self-service place with trays behind a glass counter. However, once-sharp dividing lines are now blurred and it's not unusual to find upmarket places calling themselves an *osteria*.

An Italian breakfast is traditionally just espresso or cappuccino with a croissant or brioche, but lunches and especially dinners can be drawn-out affairs of 2 hours or more. The classic Tuscan *antipasti* or appetizers are crostini and cured meats such as prosciutto and salami, often served with *pecorino* (sheep's milk) cheese. *Antipasti di mare* is a mixed seafood starter popular by the coast. *Panzanella* is a filling summer salad of stale bread and olive oil with tomato and garlic.

A *primo* or first course will probably be pasta, such as *pappardelle alla lepre* (ribbon pasta with hare) or *al cinghiale* (with wild boar). *Pici* (rough, hand-rolled spaghetti) is typical of southern Tuscany. Tuscan soups include *pappa al pomodoro* (thick tomato and bread soup) and hearty *ribollita*.

The *secondo* or main course is usually rustic, perhaps simple roasted or spicy meat or a spicy *peposo* (beef stew). The iconic Tuscan steak is the *bistecca*, a huge T-bone sold by weight and grilled rare. *Baccalà* (salted cod) is often served alla *Livonese* (stewed with tomatoes). For dessert, most places offer *cantucci* (or *biscotti*) and Vin Santo.

Italian meals are not complete without wine – be it either *vino rosso* (red or *bianco* (white). Vernaccia di San Gimignano, Vino Nobile di Montepulciano, Morellino di Scansano, Brunello di Montalcino and Chianti are the top Tuscan zones (see pp40–41 and pp70–71).

The restaurant *pane e coperto* cover charge is unavoidable. If the menu says "*servizio incluso*" (or the waiter confirms so when you ask, "*E' incluso il servizio?*"), service is included. Locals rarely leave anything extra, but it's customary for foreign visitors to round up by a few euros if service has been good. In most places, waiters expect you to linger over a meal and won't rush you.

In the unlikely event that you are struggling to find somewhere to eat in Florence, **The Fork** has user reviews and a booking function for a wide range of restaurants in the city.

Where to Stay

Hotels are categorized from 1 (basic) to 5 (deluxe) stars, based on amenities rather than charm or location. At 3 stars and above, all rooms have at least a private bathroom. **Citalia** has a good selection of Florence hotel packages.

Working farms – often vineyards – offer lodgings in bucolic settings. Some are luxury, some rustic and inexpensive. Local tourist boards have lists of these *agriturismi*, as do the consortiums **Terra Nostra** and **Agriturist**. **Sawday's** offers a curated collection of upper-range *agriturismi*, alongside rural apartments, unique small hotels and B&Bs.

A private villa in the Tuscan hills is the stuff of holiday dreams. Agencies with good property portfolios include **CV Villas**, **To Tuscany**, **Cottages to Castles**, **Insider's Italy**, **Tuscany Now** and **Parker Villas**. **GoWithOh** and **Cross Pollinate** have apartments in Florence.

For budget travellers, most tourist offices keep a list of *affittacamere* (cheap room rentals), which can range from semi-private access and a lovely room to a cramped spare room in someone's apartment. There's always **Airbnb**, too.

Ostelli Online is good for finding hostels. Most tend to be on the edges of towns. **Monastery Stays** books rooms in religious houses across Tuscany and in central Florence. Services and facilities can be quite basic, but the whole experience is very atmospheric. Note that curfews of 11pm or earlier often apply.

The best-known Tuscan hotels can book up months in advance. Florence tends to be very full at Easter, through May and June, and during Pitti Uomo fashion weeks (mid-January and mid-June). At other times, you should have little problem finding a room.

Beach resorts are packed across July and August. Florence, by contrast, is empty of locals in August, although tourism keeps the place busy year-round (still, you might find a last-minute August deal in the centre).

Mainstream booking engines **Hotels.com** and **Booking.com** offer choices all over Tuscany, although it is often worthwhile contacting the hotel to haggle, because they'll save on commission if you book direct. You may need patience waiting for a reply to emails. The **Hotel Tonight** app and website often lists last-minute rooms at big discounts.

Rooms without private baths or views, or for stays longer than three days, are usually cheaper. An extra bed costs around 30 per cent more (sometimes free for under-14s in the parents' room). Breakfast may not be included but if you are in a town, it's usually not worth paying the extra if you have the option. Parking will usually cost extra in towns, but rarely in rural hotels. Minibar prices and phone call charges are almost always exorbitant.

DIRECTORY

SHOPPING

Madova
w madova.com

DINING

The Fork
w thefork.it

WHERE TO STAY

Agriturist
w agriturist.it

Airbnb
w airbnb.com

Booking.com
w booking.com

Citalia
w citalia.com

Cottages to Castles
w cottagestocastles.com

Cross Pollinate
w cross-pollinate.com

CV Villas
w cvvillas.com

GoWithOh
w gowithoh.com

Hotel Tonight
w hoteltonight.com

Hotels.com
w hotels.com

Insider's Italy
w insidersitaly.com

Monastery Stays
w monasterystays.com

Ostelli Online
w ostellionline.net

Parker Villas
w parkervillas.com

Sawdays
w sawdays.co.uk

Terra Nostra
w terranostra.it

To Tuscany
w to-tuscany.com

Tuscany Now
w tuscanynow.com

Places to Stay

PRICE CATEGORIES

For a standard, double room per night (with breakfast if included), taxes and extra charges.

€ under €100   €€ €100–200   €€€ over €200

Luxury Hotels

Aia Mattonata, outside Siena

MAP E4 ▪ Strada del Ceraiolo 1, Doglia ▪ 0577 392 073 ▪ Wi-Fi ▪ www.aiamattonata.com ▪ €€€

The five charming rooms in this converted farmhouse – whose oldest parts date from the 7th century – have a romantic feel, with muted pastel shades and canopy beds (in some). All the rooms have air conditioning and en suite bathrooms. The hotel boasts a lovely outdoor pool, and is well placed to explore Siena, Montalcino and Pienza. There is a two-night minimum stay. Children over 12 are welcome.

Belmond Villa San Michele, Fiesole

MAP E2 ▪ Via Doccia 4 ▪ 055 567 8200 ▪ Wi-Fi ▪ www.belmond.com/villa-san-michele-florence ▪ €€€

Michelangelo is said to have designed the façade of this 15th-century former Franciscan monastery that stands between Florence and Fiesole. The original building has only double rooms, with the sumptuous suites hiding in half-buried wings overlooking the terraced gardens and heated pool. The large wooded park has a walking trail, and there is also a gym.

Castiglion del Bosco, near Montalcino

MAP E4 ▪ Loc Castiglion del Bosco ▪ 0577 191 3001 ▪ Wi-Fi ▪ www.castigliondelbosco.com ▪ €€€

Situated in the beautiful Val d'Orcia (a UNESCO World Heritage Site) in the Brunello di Montalcino wine region, this resort stands next to the pilgrim route of Via Francigena. The 800-year-old rural estate has been transformed into a chic hideaway with a heated infinity pool, a spa, a golf course and a winery. Rooms and suites are in the old Borgo, and 17th- and 18th-century stone farmhouses are now luxury villas with private, heated pools. The views are sublime.

Four Seasons, Florence

MAP Q1 ▪ Borgo Pinti 99 ▪ 055 26 261 ▪ Wi-Fi ▪ www.fourseasons.com/florence ▪ €€€

A genuine Renaissance palace surrounded by one of the largest private gardens in Florence and boasting a spa and an outdoor pool, the Four Seasons is the ultimate city retreat. The rooms and suites range from the large and luxurious to the downright palatial, some retaining original frescoes and expertly restored stucco work. The service is five-star.

Gallia Palace, Punta Ala

MAP D5 ▪ Punta Ala ▪ 0564 922 022 ▪ Wi-Fi ▪ www.galliapalace.it ▪ €€€

The top hotel in Tuscany's most exclusive coastal resort, the Gallia Palace has large, tasteful rooms, a beauty spa, a swimming pool in the park, a private beach with boats and canoes and access to a neighbouring golf course. Weekend candlelit dinners take place on the hotel's lawn.

Helvetia e Bristol, Florence

MAP M3 ▪ Via de Pescioni 2 ▪ 055 26 651 ▪ Wi-Fi ▪ www.hotelhelvetia bristol.com ▪ €€€

Although lacking all the amenities at the Excelsior and Villa San Michele's setting, the Helvetia still feels posher than either. The most central of the city's luxury hotels, this has been operating since the 19th century and has welcomed distinguished guests, including composer Igor Stravinsky and writer Bertrand Russell.

Il Pellicano, Monte Argentario

MAP E6 ▪ Loc Lo Sbarcatello ▪ 0564 858 111 ▪ Wi-Fi ▪ www.pellicanohotel.com ▪ €€€

An oasis of luxury on a wild and scenic bit of the Maremma coast, the original house was built by American socialites Patricia and Michael Graham for themselves and their friends. Now an exclusive hotel with a delightful hint of retro atmosphere, Il Pellicano consists of a villa and cottages among cypress, pine and olive woods. Amenities include a piano bar, gym, tennis courts, a heated seawater pool, spa and water-skiing facilities.

Villa Ottone, Elba

MAP C5 ▪ Loc Ottone ▪ 0565 933 042 ▪ www.villaottone.com ▪ €€€
This is the classiest place to stay on Elba, especially if you have a room in the original 19th-century villa. But even the 1970s main building has terraces with sea views. There's also a spa offering Turkish baths, Ayurveda treatments and Thai massage, plus a pool, tennis court and water-sports equipment.

Villa Scacciapensieri, outside Siena

MAP E4 ▪ Via Scacciapensieri 10 ▪ 0577 41 441 ▪ www.villa scacciapensieri.it ▪ €€€
Set in a 19th-century villa just outside Siena overlooking the city walls in hilly parkland, the villa has spacious rooms, including three suites. Meals are served on the terraces, and there are tennis courts and a pool. The hotel is also perfectly placed to allow you to both enjoy Siena (whose historic core is only a few kilometres away) and to savour the beautiful countryside and views of the hills of Chianti.

Westin Excelsior, Florence

MAP K3 ▪ Piazza Ognissanti 3 ▪ 055 27 151 ▪ Wi-Fi ▪ www.westin florence.com ▪ €€€
The top address in town, this is a bastion of luxury and refinement set in a Renaissance palace on the Arno. There are few amenities that the hotel lacks or services it cannot provide. In-room spa treatments are available, and you can book a room equipped with a treadmill or stationary bike. Try to get an Arno-side room. The penthouse rooms have stunning views of the Duomo and the river.

Historic Hotels

L'Antico Pozzo, San Gimignano

MAP D3 ▪ Via San Matteo 87 ▪ 0577 942 014 ▪ Wi-Fi ▪ www.anticopozzo.com ▪ €€
Although predominantly 15th century, bits of the building date back to the Middle Ages. Its name comes from an ancient well on the site that was used, the story goes, to hang young women who resisted the medieval *droit de seigneur* law. In the 17th century it hosted Inquisition trials. Large rooms and iron bedsteads lend an antique air, while the "superior" rooms come with the original 17th-century frescoes.

Hotel della Fortezza, Sorano

MAP F5 ▪ Piazza Cairoli 5 ▪ 0564 633 549 ▪ Closed Jan & Feb ▪ www.hotel dellafortezza.com ▪ €€
This 16-room hotel is installed in a wing of Sorano's 11th-century Fortezza degli Orsini *(see p129)*. The comfortable rooms come with wooden ceilings, 19th-century furnishings and fantastic countryside views. With the high breezes flowing through here, there is no need for air conditioning.

Palazzo Ravizza, Siena

MAP E4 ▪ Pian de Mantellini 34 ▪ 0577 280 462 ▪ Wi-Fi ▪ www.palazzoravizza.it ▪ €€
A family-run 17th-century hotel. Some rooms retain their frescoes, and those at the back are quiet and offer garden views.

Royal Victoria, Pisa

MAP C3 ▪ Lungarno Pacinotti 12 ▪ 050 940 111 ▪ Wi-Fi ▪ www.royalvictoria.it ▪ €€
Opened in 1839, Pisa's oldest hotel has had John Ruskin and Theodore Roosevelt as guests. It is not as grand as it once was, but still oozes history and has a prime location on the Arno. Some doubles link to make family suites, and there's a private parking garage for guests.

Villa de' Fiori, near Pistoia

MAP D2 ▪ Via di Bigiano e Castel Bovani 39 ▪ 0573 450 351 ▪ Wi-Fi ▪ www.villadefiori.it ▪ €€
This patrician villa-hotel dating from the 1600s is on the city outskirts, amid farms and olive groves in the Pistoiese hills. Rooms are stuffed with antiques – it feels as if the *Contessa* has just popped out. Enjoy a dip in the outdoor pool.

Albergo Pietrasanta, Pietrasanta

MAP C2 ▪ Via Garibaldi 35 ▪ 0584 793 726 ▪ www.albergo pietrasanta.com ▪ €€€
This 17th-century palazzo is an exclusive hotel, with baths sheathed in the marbles of this mining town between Forte dei Marmi and Viareggio.

Loggiato dei Serviti, Florence
MAP P2 ▪ Piazza Santissima Annunziata 3 ▪ 055 289 592 ▪ www.loggiatodeiservitihotel.it ▪ €€€
High Renaissance-styled rooms in a 1527 building designed by Antonio da Sangallo the Elder. The best, if slightly noisier, rooms open onto a magnificent loggia overlooking the square. Canopy beds add to the antique air.

Morandi alla Crocetta, Florence
MAP P2 ▪ Via Laura 50 ▪ 055 234 4747 ▪ Wi-Fi ▪ www.hotelmorandi.it ▪ €€€
Built as a convent in 1511, the ten-room Morandi is located in the historic centre of the city. Some of the beams, antiques and artwork are reproductions, but the frescoes are genuine 16th century.

Villa Pitiana, Florence
MAP E3 ▪ Via Provinciale per Tosi 7 ▪ 055 860 259 ▪ Wi-Fi ▪ www.villapitiana.com ▪ €€€
This much-altered former monastery, in a park on the outskirts of Florence, has hosted Galileo and Petrarch. Decent restaurant and outdoor pool.

Villa di STR, Siena
MAP E4 ▪ Viale Vittorio Veneto 11 ▪ 0577 188 2807 ▪ www.lavilladistr.it ▪ €€€
In an Art Nouveau-style villa located just outside the city walls, this boutique hotel has a lovely garden and many rooms have private balconies. It is noted for its hearty breakfasts.

Comfortable Hotels

Albergo Duomo, Montepulciano
MAP F4 ▪ Via San Donato 14 ▪ 0578 757 473 ▪ www.albergoduomo montepulciano.it ▪ €
This family-run inn just steps from the Duomo adds rustic accents such as wooden dressers and iron bedsteads to the modern decor. There's a small courtyard for summer breakfasts.

Antiche Mura, Arezzo
MAP F3 ▪ Piaggia di Murello 35 ▪ 0575 20 410 ▪ Wi-Fi ▪ www.antiche mura.info ▪ €
The shell is old Tuscany but inside are six bright, flamboyant rooms individually decorated and named after women from history and the arts, including Baroque painter Artemisia Gentileschi and Audrey Hepburn's Holly Golightly. Breakfast is served in a nearby café.

Patria, Pistoia
MAP D2 ▪ Via F Crispi 8 ▪ 0573 358 800 ▪ www.patriahotel.com ▪ €
Pistoia has a dearth of decent hotels, but this modern place is a good start. It boasts several amenities, including baby- and dog-sitting services, and a great location between the train station and the Duomo.

Dei Capitani, Montalcino
MAP E4 ▪ La Lapini 6 ▪ 0577 847 227 ▪ Wi-Fi ▪ www.deicapitani.it ▪ €€
Located in the historic centre of town, this was once a barracks for the Sienese army in their last stand against Florentine forces. Now its rustic rooms exude comfort and serenity, with sweeping valley views from the rooms at the back and lofted mini-apartments on the street side. There's also a small terrace pool.

Hotel San Michele, Cortona
MAP F4 ▪ Via Guelfa 15 ▪ 0575 604 348 ▪ www.hotelsanmichele.net ▪ €€
A 15th-century palazzo of High Renaissance architectural panache, with creamy plaster against soft grey stone. The hotel boasts beamed ceilings, antiques and rural vistas from many rooms, and yet is sited right in the centre of town.

Hotel Scilla, Sovana
MAP F6 ▪ Via Rodolfo Siviero 3 ▪ 0564 614 329 ▪ www.albergoscilla.com ▪ €€
In the centre of one of Tuscany's most charming villages, 15 rooms spread over three buildings mix the contemporary and the antique – exposed walls and engraved headboards vie with modern baths and glass table tops. The on-site restaurant is good, and staff are friendly.

La Luna, Lucca
MAP C2 ▪ Via Filungo, Corte Compagni 12 ▪ 0583 493 634 ▪ www.hotellaluna.com ▪ €€
This family-run hotel is located in a quiet cul-de-sac off Lucca's main shopping street. The rooms are split between two buildings; most furnishings are modern, but try to get a second-floor room in the older half of the hotel, which retain some original 17th-century frescoes.

Pensione Pendini, Florence

MAP M3 ▪ Via Strozzi 2 ▪ 055 211 170 ▪ Wi-Fi ▪ www.hotelpendini.it ▪ €€

Little has changed here for over 120 years, save the addition of firm beds and new furnishings. The larger rooms overlooking Piazza della Reppublica are best. The Abbolafaio brothers' welcome is warm, and they have two other hotels in town (one near the station, the other on the Arno).

Santa Caterina, Siena

MAP E4 ▪ Via Enea Silvio Picolomini 7 ▪ 0577 221 105 ▪ Wi-Fi ▪ www.hotel santacaterinasiena.com ▪ €€

There is plenty of oak and manor-house-style fittings in the rooms. Those facing south have unforgettable views over the hills south of Siena.

Davanzati, Florence

MAP M4 ▪ Via Porta Rossa 5 ▪ 055 286 666 ▪ Wi-Fi ▪ www.hotel davanzati.it ▪ €€€

Family-run hotel on a medieval street in the historic core. Rooms are decorated in traditional Tuscan style, with terracotta floors, including in several family rooms. The friendly hosts offer a daily free aperitif happy hour.

Budget Gems

Bernini, Siena

MAP E4 ▪ Via della Sapienza 15 ▪ 0577 289 047 ▪ www.albergo-bernini.com ▪ €

A tiny, family-run hotel that books up quickly. The nine whitewashed rooms atop the convent of St Catherine are quiet. Two have views of the Duomo, two have air conditioning and four are en suite.

Il Colombaio, Castellina in Chianti

MAP E3 ▪ Via Chiantigiana 29 ▪ 0577 740 444 ▪ www.albergo ilcolombaio.it ▪ €

This converted farmhouse has retained a strong country air, with rustic antiques and bucolic vistas. Large rooms open off cosy lounges. There's also a small pool.

La Dimora del Corso, Montepulciano

MAP F4 ▪ Via di Gracciano nel Corso ▪ 0388 045 0020 ▪ Wi-Fi ▪ www.trattoriadi cagnano.it ▪ €

Halfway up the main street, just steps from the 16th-century Torre di Pulcinella (a Neapolitan character analogous to the British Mr Punch) is this three-floored B&B. The eight rooms (some with terraces) have been recently renovated, with air conditioning and elevator access. The friendly owners have another B&B, a restaurant and three apartments nearby.

Locanda Orchidea, Florence

MAP P3 ▪ Via Borgo degli Albizi 11 ▪ 333 837 9256 ▪ Wi-Fi ▪ www.locanda orchidea.it ▪ €

Simply decorated rooms with cool tiled floors and private bathrooms are tucked away in the shuttered 13th-century Palazzo Donati, whose facade was designed by Buontalenti. It is thought that Dante's wife, Gemma Donati, was born here. The rooms at the back overlook a quiet, leafy courtyard. The English owner is a good source of city information.

Locanda del Vino Nobile, near Montepulciano

MAP F4 ▪ Via dei Lillà 1, Sant' Albino di Montepulciano ▪ 0578 798 064 ▪ Wi-Fi ▪ www.lalocanda delvinonobile.it ▪ €

This B&B offers five rooms with terracotta tiles and wooden ceilings, set above an excellent Tuscan restaurant. Breakfast is an event, with fresh fruit and home-baked cakes. The roadside location is ideal for those touring the countryside by car.

Piccolo Hotel Etruria, Siena

MAP E4 ▪ Vicolo Donzelle 3 ▪ 0577 288 088 ▪ www.hoteletruria.com ▪ €

In a centre plagued by either overpriced or grotty hotels, tiny Etruria stands proud. In a 16th-century building close to Piazza del Campo, its 13 immaculate rooms with contemporary decor are great value and very popular. The only drawback is the 1am curfew. Book early.

Piccolo Hotel Puccini, Lucca

MAP C2 ▪ Via di Poggio 9 ▪ 0583 55 421 ▪ www.hotelpuccini.com ▪ €

In this very friendly hotel, all but two of the smallish but nicely furnished rooms are on the front. If you lean out, you can see the Romanesque façade of San Michele.

For a key to hotel price categories see p142

Porta Castellana, Montalcino

MAP E4 ▪ Via Santa Lucia 20 ▪ 0577 839 001 ▪ Wi-Fi ▪ www.portacastellana.it ▪ €

Three B&B rooms crafted out of a former storehouse with barrel-vaulted ceilings. It has all been designed with a keen eye and good taste. Breakfast is brought to your room or served in a garden with views over the Val d'Orcia.

Vizi Ottavo, Castiglion Fiorentino

MAP F4 ▪ Via San Michele 69 ▪ 0575 657 319 ▪ Wi-Fi ▪ www.viziottavo.com ▪ €

The "eighth vice" B&B has bold-coloured rooms with chromatherapy showers, each styled after one of the seven deadly sins. Second-floor rooms Ira (Anger) and Invidia (Envy) have terraces. The honeymoon suite (Lust, of course) has great views.

Italia, Cortona

MAP F4 ▪ Via Ghibellina 5/7 ▪ 0575 630 254 ▪ www.hotelitaliacortona. com ▪ €€

Just a few steps off the main piazza, the Italia offers standard comforts and modern furnishings. A few rooms have views of the countryside beyond Cortona's rooftops.

Agriturismi

Fattoria Castello di Verrazzano, Greve in Chianti

MAP E3 ▪ Via Citille 32A, Loc Greti ▪ 055 854 243 ▪ Closed Jan & Feb ▪ www. verrazzano.com ▪ €

A 12th-century castle and wine estate that offers seven rooms (minimum three nights) and two apartments (weekly). Cantina visits and wine tastings available, and the restaurant is good.

Podere Marcampo, near Volterra

MAP D3 ▪ Loc S Cipriano 30 ▪ 0588 85 393 ▪ Wi-Fi ▪ www.agriturismo- marcampo.com ▪ €

Modern-rustic rooms and apartments in a pristine stone farmhouse with an outdoor pool and stunning views back to Volterra. The estate's own wines are excellent. Half board is available at Volterra's Del Duca restaurant (see p119), which is owned by the same family.

Podere Terreno, Radda in Chianti

MAP E3 ▪ Strada per Volpaia ▪ 0577 057 719 ▪ www.podereterreno.it ▪ €

The welcome is warm at this old, family-run countryside smallholding of seven rustic rooms with original features. Unlike most agriturismi, you dine with the hosts and other guests at a long table.

Il Cicalino, Massa Marittima

MAP D4/5 ▪ Loc Cicalino ▪ 0566 902 031 ▪ www.ilcicalino.it ▪ €€

This complex of converted buildings in a farm/park offers 12 doubles and nine triples, a Tuscan restaurant, pool, football pitch and gym. Mountain-bike rental is available. Minimum three nights.

Fattoria Maionchi, Lucca

MAP C2 ▪ Loc Tofori ▪ 0583 978 194 ▪ www. fattoriamaionchi.it ▪ €€

The four large, multilevel apartments, sleeping four to six, are country-styled and set in pretty gardens. The minimum stay is three nights in low season.

Grazia, Orbetello

MAP E6 ▪ Via Aurelia 4/b ▪ 0564 881 182 ▪ www. agriturismograzia.com ▪ €€

This 18th-century villa is surrounded by apartments that sleep two to four people. Guided horse rides are available and the nature reserves are close by. There's also a pool and tennis courts. Three nights minimum.

Tenuta Castello il Corno, San Casciano

MAP E3 ▪ Malafrasca 64 ▪ 055 824 851 ▪ Closed Jan & Feb ▪ Wi-Fi ▪ www. tenutailcorno.com ▪ €€

Ten apartments and six rooms are available in former peasant quarters around a fine vineyard villa. You can also learn Tuscan cooking. Three-night minimum stay.

I Bonsi, Reggello

MAP E3 ▪ Via I Bonsi 47, Loc Sant'Agata ▪ 0558 652 118 ▪ www.agri turismoibonsi.it ▪ €€€

A tree-lined avenue leads to this magnificent country residence set in parkland overlooking the Arno valley. There are six apartments to let. Three-night minimum stay.

Fattoria Castello di Pratelli, Incisa

MAP E3 ▪ Via di Pratelli 1A ▪ 055 833 5986 ▪ Closed Nov & Dec ▪ Wi-Fi ▪ www.castello dipratelli.it ▪ €€€

A turretted fortress from the Dark Ages with eight spacious apartments anchors this wine and olive oil estate. There's also a pool, and mountain bikes for hire. The minimum stay is two nights on weekends in low season.

Villa Vignamaggio, Greve in Chianti

MAP E3 ▪ Villa Vignamaggio ▪ 055 854 661 ▪ www.vignamaggio.com ▪ €€€

The birthplace of Mona Lisa, this 14th-century villa (see p40 and p64) and its surrounding cottages make a sumptuous *agriturismo*. The rooms are painted in strong colours, and the gardens were featured in the film *Much Ado About Nothing*. Tennis courts and two pools round it off. The apartments have Jacuzzis and cooking facilities. Minimum two nights.

Countryside Hotel Retreats

Casa Campanella, Elba

MAP C5 ▪ Piano di Mola ▪ 0565 915 740 ▪ Closed Nov–Mar ▪ Wi-Fi ▪ www.casacampanella.it ▪ €€

Modern mini-apartments in large grounds with an outdoor pool amid the quiet of the Elban countryside. Capoliveri's nightlife and the beaches at Zuccale and Barabarca are within 1.5 km (1 mile).

Castello di Gargonza, Monte San Savino

MAP F4 ▪ Loc Gargonza ▪ 0575 847 021 ▪ Wi-Fi ▪ www.gargonza.it ▪ €€

Medieval castle turned spectacular hostelry in a charming 13th-century fortified village. Although far from civilization, the Castello di Gargonza, with its fine restaurant, and a

pool just outside the village walls, feels less removed than many a rural retreat. Both rooms and self-catering apartments are available.

Castello Ripa d'Orcia, San Quirico d'Orcia

MAP F4 ▪ Loc Ripa d'Orcia ▪ 0577 897 376 ▪ www.castelloripa dorcia.com ▪ €€

A fairy-tale hotel hewn from a 13th-century castle and outbuildings immersed in the green hills of a nature reserve. Relaxation is the order of your stay, with an absence of TVs and telephones in the huge, country-styled rooms and apartments.

Relais San Pietro, Castiglion Fiorentino

MAP F4 ▪ Loc Polvano 3 ▪ 0575 650 100 ▪ Open Mar–Oct ▪ Wi-Fi ▪ www.polvano.com ▪ €€

A delightful 17th-century farmhouse, this is in an idyllic location overlooking a valley. Accommodation is either in the main building or a converted priest's house. The decor is typically Tuscan. Dinner is often served on the terrace in summer.

Villa Rosa in Boscorotondo, Panzano

MAP E3 ▪ Via San Leolino 65 ▪ 055 852 577 ▪ www.resortvillarosa.it ▪ €€

This isolated villa stands on a thickly forested stretch of Chianti roadside. The spacious rooms feature beamed ceilings and, for those on the front, access to two large terraces. There's a pool, woodland trails and excellent set dinners on the terrace in summer.

Castello di Spaltenna, Gaiole

MAP E3 ▪ Castello di Spaltenna ▪ 0577 749 483 ▪ Wi-Fi ▪ www.spaltenna.it ▪ €€€

Around the core of a 12th-century castle, this is the Chianti's most luxurious inn. It has a room for wine tasting, an outdoor pool and a plethora of antiques. Corner rooms, with their ceiling beams, are best.

Locanda dell' Amorosa, Sinalunga

MAP F4 ▪ Loc L'Amorosa ▪ 0577 677 211 ▪ Wi-Fi ▪ www.amorosa.it ▪ €€€

The "Lover's Inn" moniker dates back to the hotel's 14th-century origins. The apartment-like accommodation has a refined rustic style under the more formal brick loggias around the courtyard.

Tenuta di Ricavo, Castellina

MAP E3 ▪ Loc Ricavo 4 ▪ 0577 740 221 ▪ Open Easter–Oct ▪ www.ricavo.com ▪ €€€

A medieval hamlet rebuilt after World War II. Now a select few can rent its 23 perfectly rusticated rooms and suites. Guests gather around a fire in winter or the pool in summer.

Villa La Massa, Candeli

MAP E3 ▪ Via della Massa 24 ▪ 055 62 611 ▪ Closed Nov–Mar ▪ www.villa lamassa.com ▪ €€€

Everyone from Churchill to Madonna has stayed in this Renaissance villa turned hotel. Tennis courts, a pool and a Tuscan restaurant overlooking the Arno justify its prestigious reputation.

For a key to hotel price categories see p142

Villa La Principessa, near Lucca

MAP C2 ▪ Via Nuova per Pisa 1616/G, Loc Massa Pisana ▪ 0583 370 963 ▪ Wi-Fi ▪ www.hotel principessalucca.it ▪ €€€
This was once the court of the 12th-century Duke of Lucca. The rooms are large and comfortable, and there is a swimming pool and garden.

Hotels with a View

Le Cetinelle, near Greve in Chianti

MAP E3 ▪ Via Canonica 13 ▪ 055 854 4745 ▪ Wi-Fi ▪ www.cetinelle.com ▪ €
Watch the sky turn pink as a hazy sun sinks into the hills above Greve from this isolated farmhouse B&B with an outdoor pool. Individually themed Tuscan rooms (none are air conditioned) do the spectacular setting justice. Wi-Fi is available.

Antica Dimora Johlea, Florence

MAP E3 ▪ Via San Gallo 80 ▪ 055 463 3292 ▪ Wi-Fi ▪ www.johanna.it ▪ €€
No Florence hotel in this price bracket has such a spectacular terrace, looking across the tiled rooftops to Brunelleschi's dome. The interiors are decked out like a stylish Florentine home (or *dimora*), with parquet floors, dark wood and busy patterns. Wi-Fi is available for guests.

La Cisterna, San Gimignano

MAP D3 ▪ Piazza della Cisterna ▪ 0577 940 328 ▪ www.hotelcisterna.it ▪ €€
You can pick your views at this hotel – front rooms have a view of the piazza

and the town's famous towers, the back rooms look over vineyards and hills. A cinematographers' favourite, the hotel put in an appearance in *Tea with Mussolini* and *Where Angels Fear to Tread*.

Il Giglio, Montalcino

MAP E4 ▪ Via Soccorso Saloni 5 ▪ 0577 848 167 ▪ www.gigliohotel.com ▪ €€
Only the eight rooms at the back enjoy the best view in town – a slope down to Tuscany's countryside on one side and cliff-hugging houses on the other. This hotel adds a touch of class to the rustic ambience.

Hotel Bigallo, Florence

MAP M3 ▪ Vicolo degli Adimari 2 ▪ 055 216 086 ▪ www.hotelbigallo florence.com ▪ €€
Located in the very heart of Florence's historic core, near the Duomo, the family-run Bigallo has long been famous among budget-conscious travellers for its views of the magnificent cathedral group. The only drawback here is the noise of passing pedestrians.

Hotel Duomo, Siena

MAP E4 ▪ Via Stalloreggi 38 ▪ 0577 289 088 ▪ www.hotelduomo.it ▪ €€
Although the palazzo dates from the 12th century, the rooms – some medium-sized, others a bit cramped – are modern and comfortable. The 12 "panoramic" rooms that feature Duomo views include a small top-floor double room with windows on three sides and sweeping vistas of Siena.

Montorio, Montepulciano

MAP F4 ▪ Strada per Pienza 2 ▪ 0578 717 442 ▪ Closed Dec–Feb ▪ Wi-Fi ▪ www.montorio.com ▪ €€
This small hilltop hotel consists of comfortable mini-apartments. The garden has the best views of the Tempio di San Biagio; all rooms have rural vistas. Minimum stay three nights.

Torre Guelfa, Florence

MAP M4 ▪ Borgo SS Apostoli 8 ▪ 055 239 6338 ▪ Wi-Fi ▪ www.hoteltorre guelfa.com ▪ €€
While most rooms in this converted 1280 palazzo don't have great views, the lofty terrace bar has an unbeatable panorama across Florence. Wi-Fi is available in the hotel.

Villa Kinzica, Pisa

MAP C3 ▪ Piazza Arcivescovado 2 ▪ 050 560 419 ▪ www.hotel villakinzica.com ▪ €€
Although the hotel is nothing special, if you get a room on the front or left side you will open your shutters on a postcard view of the Leaning Tower. However, only half the hotel's rooms have air conditioning.

Torre di Bellosguardo, Florence

MAP E3 ▪ Via Roti Michelozzi 2 ▪ 055 229 8145 ▪ www.torrebellos guardo.com ▪ €€€
The views from Fiesole are famous, but the panorama from Bellosguardo hill above the Oltrarno is better – a close-up sweep of the Florence skyline from the gardens and

pool of an evocatively medieval retreat. The central tower contains a suite which features unsurpassed views in all four directions.

Monasteries and Youth Hostels

Abbazia di Monte Oliveto Maggiore

MAP E4 ■ Abbazia di Monte Oliveto Maggiore ■ 0577 707 652 ■ Closed Nov ■ No credit cards ■ www.monteoliveto maggiore.it ■ €

This gorgeously frescoed monastery in the hills offers single and double rooms with private baths, and also sells honey, herbs and wines. The drive to the monastery is a Tuscan classic.

Foresteria Volterra, Volterra

MAP D4 ■ Loc San Girolamo ■ 0588 80 050 ■ Wi-Fi ■ www.foresteria volterra.it ■ €

This purpose-built hostel, located in the woods just outside the eastern gates of Volterra, has spacious modern rooms, from singles to quads. The rooms are all private and have en suite bathrooms and a small private outdoor terrace.

Ostello Apuano, Marina di Massa

MAP C2 ■ Viale delle Pinete, Partaccia 237 ■ 0585 780 034 ■ www. ostelloapuano.com ■ Open Mar–Sep ■ €

Set in a coastal park, this villa-hostel offers bike rental, a beach and plenty of park to enjoy. The family rooms are not available from July to August. 11:30pm curfew.

Ostello Archi Rossi, Florence

MAP M2 ■ Via Faenza 94r ■ 055 290 804 ■ Wi-Fi ■ www.hostelarchirossi. com ■ €

This popular, well-located hostel caters to families, individuals and groups. It has good facilities, although not all rooms have a private bathroom.

Ostello del Chianti, Tavernelle Val di Pesa

MAP E3 ■ Via Roma 137 ■ 055 805 0265 ■ Closed Nov–Mar ■ www. ostellodelchianti.it ■ €

The activities here are geared toward wine production and tasting. The hostel has a few family rooms. Breakfasts and packed lunches are available at an extra cost. SITA buses stop nearby.

Ostello San Frediano, Lucca

MAP C2 ■ Via della Cavallerizza 12 ■ 0583 496 976 ■ www.ostello lucca.it ■ €

A converted convent located outside the town walls (take buses 59, 60, 3 or Navetta 2), with dorms and family rooms, some with private bathrooms.

Plus Florence, Florence

MAP E3 ■ Via Santa Caterina d'Alessandria 15 ■ 055 628 6347 ■ Wi-Fi ■ www.plushostels.com ■ €

This is billed as a hostel, but has better facilities than most pricey city hotels, including an outdoor pool (summer), an indoor pool and a Turkish bath (winter only). Private rooms in the new building have the best furnishings. All are en suite.

Santuario San Caterina/Alma Domus, Siena

MAP E4 ■ Via Camporeggio 37 ■ 0577 44 177 ■ www.hotelalma domus.it ■ €

The nuns of St Catherine run this simple but comfortable inn. Many of the rooms have great views across a narrow valley to the striped Duomo. All the rooms have phones (receiving incoming calls only) and air conditioning. There's a television lounge and pay phones in the common rooms.

Villa I Cancelli, Florence

MAP E2 ■ Via Incontri 21 ■ 055 422 6001 ■ No credit cards ■ €

This 15th-century palazzo is set in the hills above Florence, a 15-minute drive from the centre of town. There are lovely rural views from the 31 simple bedrooms or the charming garden. The gates shut at 11pm, although the sisters will reopen them to let you back in later if need be.

Suore Oblate dell'Assunzione, Florence

MAP P3 ■ Borgo Pinti 15 ■ 055 248 0582 ■ Wi-Fi ■ www.monasterystays. com ■ €€

A Medici-era palace, this is now run by nuns as a peaceful guesthouse. The rooms are basic but comfortable and spacious, and the sisters are very welcoming. It is also right in the centre: almost everything major in the city is within walking distance from the front door. There is a minimum stay of two nights.

For a key to hotel price categories see p142

Index

Acknowledgments

Reid Bramblett

Reid has authored or contributed to over 30 guidebooks, including the *DK Eyewitness Top 10 Travel Guide: Milan & the Lakes* and many of Frommer's guides to Italy. He is also frequent contributor to well-known travel magazines and online publications.

Additional contributor
Donald Strachan

Publishing Director Georgina Dee

Publisher Vivien Antwi

Design Director Phil Ormerod

Editorial Ankita Awasthi-Tröger, Michelle Crane, Rebecca Flynn, Rachel Fox, Cincy Jose, Freddie Marriage, Fíodhna Ní Ghríofa, Scarlett O'Hara, Sally Schafer, Hollie Teague

Design Tessa Bindloss, Richard Czapnik, Rahul Kumar

Commissioned Photography Dan Bannister, John Heseltine,Rough Guides/Michelle Grant, Rough Guides/Chris Hutty, Rough Guides/Roger Mapp, Rough Guides/James McConnachie, Kim Sayer, Helena Smith, Clive Streeter, Kellie Walsh, Christine Webb, Linda Whitwam

Picture Research Susie Peachey, Ellen Root, Lucy Sienkowska, Oran Tarjan

Cartography Zafar ul Islam Khan, Suresh Kumar, Casper Morris

DTP Jason Little, George Nimmo

Production Olivia Jeffries

Factchecker Frederico Damonte

Proofreader Samantha Cook

Indexer Hilary Bird

Illustrator Chris Orr & Associates

Revisions Marcella Simoni, Rachel Thompson, Vinita Venugopal

First edition created by Blue Island Publishing, London

Picture Credits

The publisher would like to thank the following for their kind permission to reproduce their photographs:
(**Key**: a-above; b-below/bottom; c-centre; f-far; l-left; r-right; t-top)

4Corners: SIME/Pietro Canali 62-3.

Abergaccio: 93br.

Alamy Images: age fotostock/José Antonio Moreno 121b; hemis.fr/ Rene Mattes 29tl, 40br, 42-3, 45cr, 122tl; imageBROKER 107br, / Jose Antonio Moreno Castellano 70b; Jam World Images 60cb; Raimund Kutter 64b; odgephoto.com/Mathew Lodge 38br; LOOK Die Bildagentur der Fotografen GmbH/Franz Marc Frei 41b; David Lyons 27crb, 65tl, 108tl; Marka 97cl, /Alberto Fornasari 76t, / massimiliano bonatti 71cl; MBP-Italia 123tl; Kimberly Mufferi 11cl; Odyssey-Images 45b; Painting 15bl; Alex Ramsay 67tr; Realy Easy Star/Toni Spagone 105tl; Guido Alberto Rossi 128-9b; Jack Sullivan 68cb; The Art Archive/Collection Dagli Orti 33b; Domenico Tondini 68t; Travel/Paul Sampson 46-7; Christine Webb 92tl; Zoonar GmbH/Jamie Watson 71tr.

AWL Images: Danita Delimont Stock 1, 3tl, 78-9; Hemis 3tr, 132-3; Francesco Iacobelli 4crb; Travel Pix Collection 22-3.

Bridgeman Images: De Agostini Picture Library/A. Dagli Orti 69cl.

Castello di Fonterutoli: Arrigo Coppitz 41tr.

Corbis: 10cra, 14tl, 17bc, 34cla, 36t; Alinari Archives/Mauro Magliani 95br; Stefano Amantini 99tl; Arte & Immagini srl 21b; Atlantide Phototravel 92cr, /Guido Cozzi 65cr, 67b, 115br, /Massimo Borchi 58t; DPA /Rolf Haid 74tl; Rose Hartman 80tr; Hemis/René Mattes 66t; Henglein and Steets 7cr; imageBROKER/Gunther Willinger 130tl; JAI/Doug Pearson 95tl; Leemage 18br, 37b, 44cb, 50tl, 51tr, 55cl; David Pollack 110cb; Vittoriano Rastelli 74b; Reuters/Tony Gentile 103br; Robert Harding World Imagery /Hans-Peter Merten 4b, /Bruno Morandi 89br; Paul Seheult 2tl, 8-9; Sylvain Sonnet 10crb, 54tr; Splash News/Daniele La Monaca 77bl; Summerfield Press 12br; The Art Archive/Alfredo Dagli Orti 13crb, 53clb; Velvia 6x7/SOPA RF/ Riccardo Spila 4t; W. Wirth 112bl.

Dreamstime.com: Abxyz 30br; Massimiliano Agati 104tl; Ettore Bordieri 116tl; Dan Breckwoldt 82b; Lenise Calleja 11tl; Tiziano Casalta 18-9; Roberto Caucino 69tr; Teerayut Chaisarn 11cra; Marco Ciannarella 60tl; Wessel Cirkel 39br; Claudio Giovanni Colombo 28ca, 43tl; Salvatore Conte 11c; Robert Crum 42br; Olga Demchishina 30cla; Ermess 122-3b; Freesurf69 24-5, 61cr, 115t; Martin Garnham 47tc; Wieslaw Jarek 4cla, 50crb; Javarman 35bl; Jborzicchi 76cb; Joyfull 11clb; Malgorzata Kistryn 44tr; Vladimir Korostyshevskiy 46cla; Mihai-bogdan Lazar 34-5; Yiu Tung Lee 57tl; Lianem 10br, 116b, 120c; Lornet 4clb, 81br; Lucasarts 19tl; Arnel Manalang 75tr; Stefano Marinari 90t; Maurizio Martini 26-7; Alberto Masnovo 25tr; Maudanros 31bc; Volodymyr Melnyk 128cl; Fabio Migliorucci 104-5 Krisztian Miklosy 26cl;

Milosk50 46b, 109b; Mineria6 26bc; minnystock 89t; Onigiriwords 4cl, 109tr; Antonio Ribeiro 30-1; Marco Saracco 60-1, 96b; Sborisov 6cla, 6-7, 81tr; Juergen Schonnop 38-9; Shaiith 110t, 126tl, 129tl; Snake81 34bl; Paula Stanley 117tl; Stevanzz 94tl; Dariusz Szwangruber 28b; Tasstock 11br; Gianni Tonazzini 111bl;Travelpeter 127tr; Raluca Tudor 121tr; Alvaro German Vilela 56bl, 97tl; Wiktor Wojtas 25br; Zoom-zoom 16bc; Loran Zutic 24br.

Enoteca Pitti Gola e Cantina: 86tl.

Ferragamo: Guglielmo de'Micheli 85tl.

Getty Images: Bethune Carmichael 33tl; DeAgostini/G. Andreini 90cb; /A. Dagli Orti 20tl, / G. Nimatallah 12cla, 20cb, S. Vannini 54bc; DEA Picture Library 53tr,13tl, 37tl, 53tr, 59b; EyeEm/ Simon Marlow 10cb; Mondadori Portfolio 32cb, 43br; Friedrich Schmidt 91bl; Visions of Our Land 83tl.

La Grotta: 125tr.

iStockphoto.com: sborisov 100-1.

La Bottega del Rame: 124cb.

La Botteghina: Giovanni Todesca 85cb.

Ora d'Aria: 87tl.

IO Osteria Personale: 87cr.

Ristorante Enoteca "Del Duca": 119cr.

Robert Harding Picture Library: Yoko Aziz 38clb, Markus Lange 2tr, 48-9.

Romano Vireggio: 113tl.

Photo Scala, Florence: Mario Bonotto 18cla, 36clb, 55tr; Photo Opera Metropolitana Siena 14bc, 15ca, 51bl, 52b, 59c.

SuperStock: Christie's Images Ltd. 51cla; Universal Images Group/Photoservice Electa 56tr.

Cover

Front and spine - 4Corners: Pietro Canali / SIME.

Back - AWL Images: Francesco Iacobelli.

Pull Out Map Cover

4Corners: Pietro Canali / SIME.

All other images © Dorling Kindersley
For further information see:
www.dkimages.com

As a guide to abbreviations in visitor information blocks: **Adm** *= admission charge.*

Penguin Random House

Printed and bound in China

First American Edition, 2002
Published in the United States by
DK Publishing, 345 Hudson Street,
New York, New York 10014

Copyright 2002, 2018 © Dorling Kindersley Limited

A Penguin Random House Company

18 19 20 21 10 9 8 7 6 5 4 3 2 1

Reprinted with revisions 2003, 2005, 2007, 2009, 2011, 2013, 2015, 2016, 2018

Published in Great Britain
by Dorling Kindersley Limited.

A catalog record for this book is available
from the Library of Congress.

ISSN 1479-344X
ISBN 978 1 4654 6897 0

MIX
Paper from
responsible sources
FSC
www.fsc.org   FSC™ C018179

SPECIAL EDITIONS OF DK TRAVEL GUIDES

DK Travel Guides can be purchased in bulk quantities at discounted prices for use in promotions or as premiums. We are also able to offer special editions and personalized jackets, corporate imprints, and excerpts from all of our books, tailored specifically to meet your own needs.

To find out more, please contact:

in the US
specialsales@dk.com

in the UK
travelguides@uk.dk.com

in Canada
specialmarkets@dk.com

in Australia
penguincorporatesales@ penguinrandomhouse.com.au

Phrase Book

In an Emergency

Help!	Aiuto!	eye-yoo-toh
Stop!	Fermate!	fair-mah-teh
Call a doctor.	Chiama un medico.	kee-ah-mah oon meh-dee-koh
Call an ambulance.	Chiama un' ambulanza.	kee-ah-mah oon am-boo-lan-tsa
Call the police.	Chiama la polizia.	kee-ah-mah lah pol-ee-tsee-ah
Call the fire brigade.	Chiama i pompieri.	kee-ah-mah ee pom-pee-air-ee

Communication Essentials

Yes/No	Si/No	see/noh
Please	Per favore	pair fah-vor-eh
Thank you	Grazie	grah-tsee-eh
Excuse me	Mi scusi	mee skoo-zee
Hello	Buon giorno	bwon jor-noh
Goodbye	Arrivederci	ah-ree-veh-dair-chee
Good evening	Buona sera	bwon-ah sair-ah
What?	Che cosa?	keh koh-sah?
When?	Quando?	kwan-doh?
Why?	Perchè?	pair-keh?
Where?	Dove?	doh-veh?

Useful Phrases

How are you?	Come sta?	koh-meh stah?
Very well, thank you.	Molto bene, grazie.	moll-toh beh-neh grah-tsee-eh
Pleased to meet you.	Piacere di conoscerla.	pee-ah-chair-eh dee-coh-noh-shair-lah
That's fine.	Va bene.	va beh-neh
Where is/are…?	Dov'è/ Dove sono…?	dov-eh/doveh soh-noh?
How do I get to…?	Come faccio per arrivare a…?	koh-meh fah-choh pair arri-var-eh ah…?
Do you speak English?	Parla inglese?	par-lah een-gleh-zeh?
I don't understand.	Non capisco.	non ka-pee-skoh
I'm sorry.	Mi dispiace.	mee dee-spee-ah-cheh

Shopping

How much does this cost?	Quant'è, per favore?	kwan-teh pair fah-vor-eh?
I would like…	Vorrei…	vor-ray
Do you have…?	Avete…?	ah-veh-teh…?
Do you take credit cards?	Accettate carte di credito?	ah-chet-tah-teh kar-teh dee creh-dee-toh?
What time do you open /close?	A che ora apre/ chiude?	ah keh or-ah ah-preh/kee-oo-deh?
this one	questo	kweh-stoh
that one	quello	kwell-oh
expensive	caro	kar-oh
cheap	a buon prezzo	ah bwon pret-soh
size, clothes	la taglia	lah tah-lee-ah
size, shoes	il numero	eel noo-mair-oh
white	bianco	bee-ang-koh
black	nero	neh-roh
red	rosso	ross-oh
yellow	giallo	jal-loh
green	verde	vair-deh
blue	blu	bloo

Types of Shop

bakery	il forno /il panificio	eel forn-oh /eel pan-ee-fee-choh
bank	la banca	lah bang-kah
bookshop	la libreria	lah lee-breh-ree-ah
cake shop	la pasticceria	lah pas-tee-chair-ee-ah
chemist	la farmacia	lah far-mah-chee-ah
delicatessen	la salumeria	lah sah-loo-meh-ree-ah
department store	il grande magazzino	eel gran-deh mag-gad-zee-noh
grocery	alimentari	ah-lee-men-tah-ree
hairdresser	il parrucchiere	eel par-oo-kee-air-eh
ice cream parlour	la gelateria	lah jel-lah-tair-ree-ah
market	il mercato	eel mair-kah-toh
newsstand	l'edicola	leh-dee-koh-lah
post office	l'ufficio postale	loo-fee-choh pos-tah-leh
supermarket	il supermercato	eel su-pair-mair-kah-toh
tobacconist	il tabaccaio	eel tah-bak-eye-oh
travel agency	l'agenzia di viaggi	lah-jen-tsee-ah dee vee-ad-jee

Sightseeing

art gallery	la pinacoteca	lah peena-koh-teh-kah
bus stop	la fermata dell'autobus	lah fair-mah-tah dell ow-toh-booss
church	la chiesa la basilica	lah kee-eh-zah lah bah-seel-i-kah
closed for holidays	chiuso per le ferie	kee-oo-zoh pair leh fair-ee-eh
garden	il giardino	eel jar-dee-no
museum	il museo	eel moo-zeh-oh
railway station	la stazione	lah stah-tsee-oh-neh
tourist information	l'ufficio turistico	loo-fee-choh too-ree-stee-koh

Staying in a Hotel

Do you have any vacant rooms?	Avete camere libere?	ah-veh-teh kah-mair-eh lee-bair-eh?
double room	una camera doppia	oona kah-mair-ah doh-pee-ah
with double bed	con letto matrimoniale	kon let-toh mah-tree-moh nee-ah-leh
twin room	una camera con due letti	oona kah-mair ah kon doo-eh let-tee
single room	una camera singola	oona kah-mair ah sing-goh-lah
room with a bath, shower	una camera con bagno, con doccia	oona kah-mair ah kon ban-yoh, kon dot-chah
I have a reservation.	Ho fatto una prenotazione.	oh fat-toh oona preh-noh-tah tsee-oh-neh

2198231868405 1

Eating Out

Have you got a table for…?	Avete una tavola per…?	ah-veh-teh oona tah-voh-lah pair…?
I'd like to reserve a table.	Vorrei riservare una tavola.	vor-ray ree-sair-vah-reh oona tah-voh-lah
breakfast	colazione	koh-lah-tsee-oh-neh
lunch	pranzo	pran-tsoh
dinner	cena	cheh-nah
The bill, please.	Il conto, per favore.	eel kon-toh pair fah-vor-eh
waitress	cameriera	kah-mair-ee-air-ah
waiter	cameriere	kah-mair-ee-air-eh
fixed price menu	il menù a prezzo fisso	eel meh-noo ah pret-soh fee-soh
dish of the day	piatto del giorno	pee-ah-toh dell jor-no
starter	antipasto	an-tee-pass-toh
first course	il primo	eel pree-moh
main course	il secondo	eel seh-kon-doh
vegetables	contorni	eel kon-tor-noh
dessert	il dolce	eel doll-cheh
cover charge	il coperto	eel koh-pair-toh
wine list	la lista dei vini	lah lee-stah day vee-nee
glass	il bicchiere	eel bee-kee-air-eh
bottle	la bottiglia	lah bot-teel-yah
knife	il coltello	eel kol-tell-oh
fork	la forchetta	lah for-ket-tah
spoon	il cucchiaio	eel koo-kee-eye-oh

Menu Decoder

l'acqua minerale	lah-kwah mee-nair-ah-leh	mineral water
gassata/ naturale	gah-zah-tah/ nah-too-rah-leh	fizzy/ still
agnello	ah-niell-oh	lamb
aglio	al-ee-oh	garlic
al forno	al for-noh	baked
alla griglia	ah-lah greel-yah	grilled
arrosto	ar-ross-toh	roast
la birra	lah beer-rah	beer
la bistecca	lah bee-stek-kah	steak
il burro	eel boor-oh	butter
il caffè	eel kah-feh	coffee
la carne	la kar-neh	meat
carne di maiale	kar-neh dee mah-yah-leh	pork
la cipolla	la chip-oh-lah	onion
i fagioli	ee fah-joh-lee	beans
il formaggio	eel for-mad-joh	cheese
le fragole	leh frah-goh-leh	strawberries
il fritto misto	eel free-toh mees-toh	mixed fried dish
la frutta	la froot-tah	fruit
frutti di mare	froo-tee dee mah-reh	seafood
i funghi	ee foon-ghee	mushrooms
i gamberi	ee gam-bair-ee	prawns
il gelato	eel jel-lah-toh	ice cream
l'insalata	leen-sah-lah-tah	salad
il latte	eel laht-teh	milk
lesso	less-oh	boiled
il manzo	eel man-tsoh	beef
l'olio	loh-lee-oh	oil
il pane	eel pah-neh	bread
le patate	leh pah-tah-teh	potatoes

le patatine fritte	leh pah-tah-teen-eh free-teh	chips
il pepe	eel peh-peh	pepper
il pesce	eel pesh-eh	fish
il pollo	eel poll-oh	chicken
il pomodoro	eel pom-moh-dor-oh	tomato
il prosciutto cotto/crudo	eel pro-shoo-toh kot-toh/ kroo-doh	ham cooked/cured
il riso	eel ree-zoh	rice
il sale	eel sah-leh	salt
la salsiccia	lah sal-see-chah	sausage
succo d'arancia/ di limone	soo-koh dah-ran-chah/ dee lee-moh-neh	orange/lemon juice
il tè	eel teh	tea
la torta	lah tor-tah	cake/tart
l'uovo	loo-oh-voh	egg
vino bianco	vee-noh bee-ang-koh	white wine
vino rosso	vee-noh ross-oh	red wine
il vitello	eel vee-tell-oh	veal
le vongole	leh von-goh-leh	clams
lo zucchero	loh zoo-kair-oh	sugar
la zuppa	lah tsoo-pah	soup

Numbers

1	uno	oo-noh
2	due	doo-eh
3	tre	treh
4	quattro	kwat-roh
5	cinque	ching-kweh
6	sei	say-ee
7	sette	set-teh
8	otto	ot-toh
9	nove	noh-veh
10	dieci	dee-eh-chee
11	undici	oon-dee-chee
12	dodici	doh-dee-chee
13	tredici	tray-dee-chee
14	quattordici	kwat-tor-dee-chee
15	quindici	kwin-dee-chee
16	sedici	say-dee-chee
17	diciassette	dee-chah-set-teh
18	diciotto	dee-chot-toh
19	diciannove	dee-chah-noh-veh
20	venti	ven-tee
30	trenta	tren-tah
40	quaranta	kwah-ran-tah
50	cinquanta	ching-kwan-tah
60	sessanta	sess-an-tah
70	settanta	set-tan-tah
80	ottanta	ot-tan-tah
90	novanta	noh-van-tah
100	cento	chen-toh
1,000	mille	mee-leh
2,000	duemila	doo-eh mee-lah
1,000,000	un milione	oon meel-yoh-neh

Time

one minute	un minuto	oon mee-noo-toh
one hour	un'ora	oon or-ah
a day	un giorno	oon jor-noh
Monday	lunedì	loo-neh-dee
Tuesday	martedì	mar-teh-dee
Wednesday	mercoledì	mair-koh-leh-dee
Thursday	giovedì	joh-veh-dee
Friday	venerdì	ven-air-dee
Saturday	sabato	sah-bah-toh
Sunday	domenica	doh-meh-nee-kah